Bessy Ogden
from her brother
Dayton
March 18/39

Yours truly
James Nack.

# THE

# Romance of the Ring,

AND

# OTHER POEMS.

BY

JAMES NACK.

NEW YORK:
DELISSER & PROCTER, 508 BROADWAY,
1859.

Entered according to Act of Congress, in the year 1858,
By JAMES NACK,
In the Clerk's Office of the District Court of the United States for the Southern District of New York.

F. Carrick, Printer,
248 Canal Street, New York.

TO

# C. NESTELL BOVEE, Esq.

---

My Dear Sir:

There cannot be a more effectual way to connect the publication of a volume with pleasant reminiscences, than to associate it with the name of a cherished friend. It is therefore perfectly natural that I should inscribe the present volume to you as an offering of esteem and affection.

Wishing, rather than expecting, that the following pages may in part repay the gratification I have derived from yours, I indulge myself at once in a pleasure and an honor, by subscribing myself

Your Friend,

JAMES NACK.

# CONTENTS.

# MEMOIR OF JAMES NACK,

BY

GEORGE P. MORRIS.

---

WHEN genius of no common order is placed in conflict with circumstances of peculiar difficulty, it presents a subject of interesting contemplation to those who take an interest in the philosophy of the human mind. Hence the career of JAMES NACK has engaged the attention of more than one eminent writer. The elegant memoir of General WETMORE is familiar to all conversant with the literature of our country; and, in the present brief sketch, we shall, to a great extent, avail ourselves of his remarks, with a few additional particulars from other sources.

JAMES NACK is the son of a merchant of the city of New York, and was born on the fourth of January 1809. From his earliest years his attention to study and literature gave promise of future distinction. His first efforts in poetry were at so early an age, it might be said of him as of POPE,

"He lisped in numbers, for the numbers came."

But the fond expectations which his precocious talents naturally inspired among his friends and family, appeared to be suddenly destroyed by an accident, which might have been fatal to the development of genius less innate, or faculties less energetic than those with which he was endowed. He had scarcely attained his ninth year, when one day, as he was descending a flight of stairs with a little playmate in his arms, his foot slipped; in his fall he caught at the nearest article, which happened to be a heavy fire-screen; this gave way, and descending upon his head, crushed and mangled it severely, depriving him of consciousness for several weeks, and of his hearing for ever.

It is a natural consequence of a deprivation of hearing in early life, for the articulation to become gradually imperfect for want of an ear to guide its pronunciation, and NACK has not entirely escaped this misfortune. Hence, though his speech is intelligible to those who have grown up with him, and become accustomed to its peculiarities, he prefers to carry on his intercourse with others in writing. To many the loss of hearing at so early an age would have presented almost unconquerable difficulties in the pursuits of science and literature; but familiar with books from his earliest years, the spirited boy only applied with the more diligence to his studies. The result may be given in the words of the late SAMUEL L. KNAPP, who knew him intimately, and was well qualified by his own talents and attainments to appreciate those of his young friend.

"His acquirements at this early age, in the languages and all the branches of knowledge, ordinary and extraordinary, are superior to those of any young man of the same age I ever met with. There is a strength and maturity about his mind rarely to be found in those who have experienced no such deprivation as he has been visited with. His criticisms have a sagacity and shrewdness unequaled by those who were critics before he was born. He acquires a language with the most astonishing facility. No one I ever knew could do it with the same readiness, except the late learned orientalist, GEORGE BETHUNE ENGLISH. NACK unites in a degree truly astonishing, those two seemingly inconsistent qualities, *restlessness* and *perseverance.* He reads and writes, and does all things as though he had just breathed the Delphic vapor, and perseveres as though he were chained to the spot by some talismanic power.

"In a few years our gifted author will find things changing around him, and his youthful labors will become the foundation stones of a goodly edifice, in the fashioning of which he has learned the skill of a literary architect, and acquired the strength to raise a temple of imperishable fame for his own and his country's glory."

Such were the impressions and expectations that JAMES NACK inspired in his boyhood, even in the veterans of literature; and a boy of such extraordinary promise must have been remarkable under any circumstances. But when we consider the difficulties he had to surmount, we must no less admire his energy and perseverance than his talents. As General WETMORE eloquently remarks, "had not JAMES NACK been deeply imbued by nature with the vision and the faculty divine—had he not been impelled by an irresistible love and a feeling for his art, he never could have overcome the numerous and seemingly insurmountable difficulties which met him at every turn in the opening of his career. Cut off in early youth from that familiar general intercourse which sweetens the days of childhood and smoothes the path to knowledge, his sole reliance was on his own natural resources; an intellect vigorous and clear, an imagination vivid and far-reaching, and a resolution that could meet and subdue the irreparable calamity of his life."

On the publication of a volume of his poems, written

between the fourteenth and seventeenth years of his age it was hailed with wonder and admiration. One of our leading reviews, in alluding to that volume, says, "For precocity of talent and attainment under circumstances peculiarly unpropitious, JAMES NACK is an intellectual wonder. As far as known, Christendom contains nothing comparable to him. All things considered, CHATTERTON did not equal him. He has written much, and many of his productions are of a high order; all of them are marked with the rich and fervid outpourings of genius. For intensity and all that gives to poetry its highest character, they are certainly not surpassed, we think not equaled by any of the early productions of Lord BYRON, and those youthful productions of the noble bard have never received the commendations they merit. It is not too much to say of this gifted young American, that when matured by time and finished by labor, some of his future efforts in song may equal the happiest of those that have immortalized the author of Childe Harold."

Among those who took an active interest in the young poet was a distinguished member of the New York Bar, who engaged him in his office, and placed an extensive and well-selected library at his disposal. "This situation," says Colonel KNAPP, "opened a new world to him. He reveled in fresh delights, devoured books upon poetry, history, philosophy, fiction, mathematics, politics, ethics, criticism, and theology. He wrote as well as read on many of these subjects; formed a thousand theories, and tore them up root and branch for new creations."

On the departure of this gentleman for Europe, young NACK formed an engagement with another of his early friends, Mr. ASTEN, at that time Clerk of the City and County of New York, who had been among the first to notice and appreciate his abilities. He soon mastered the intricacies of the various duties required of him; and the manner in which he has fulfilled them has been well described by General WETMORE: "The dry details of legal papers, the monotonous toil of searching the musty records of the courts, however uncongenial to the poetic temperament, have no power to turn him from the path of duty. He enters thoroughly into the spirit of his various labors, and discharges them with a zeal and ability which probably few could equal, and which has secured for him not only the confidence of his successive employers, but the warm regard and esteem of the members of the Bar."

In the early part of the year 1838, Mr. NACK was united to a young lady to whom he had been attached almost from her childhood; and who, it would appear, from more than one beautiful tribute to her worth, which may rank among the happiest efforts of his pen, must have been every way worthy of his choice.

The poetry of JAMES NACK is characterized by a versification remarkably flowing, easy, and musical—an unaffected and felicitous diction—and a depth and tenderness of feeling for which he may be eminently considered the poet of the affections.

His personal qualities could not be more accurately described than in the words of General WETMORE: "Mr. NACK's habits are regular and retired. The domestic attractions of home have a greater charm for him than the allurements of the world. The amusements and excitements of society can rarely win him from his books or his desk. He is averse to mixed company, reserved in the presence of strangers, but familiar and playful in the circle of his select friends; of strong passions; quick to resent, but quicker to forgive; prone to act upon the the impulse of the moment; of a disposition gentle, generous, and sincere. He is fond of children, and successful in engaging their affections. With such qualities of mind and heart, it is not surprising that he secures the warm regard of those who have the happiness of his acquaintance, nor that he is most esteemed by those who know him best."

In conclusion, the writer cannot forbear availing himself of this opportunity to express his own high appreciation of the worth and genius of one whom it has for many years been his privilege to number among his most intimate and most esteemed friends.

Geo. P. Morris.

# ROMANCE OF THE RING.

# ROMANCE OF THE RING.

## PART FIRST.

All night he rode till the break of day,
  Nor paused he at any place;
The red blood ran on his booted heel,
  And the white foam flew in his face;
The sides of his courser heaved amain,
  The sides of his coal-black steed,
And the sweat ran down, and the smoke curled up
  Yet slackened he not his speed.
The horse and the rider, away, away!
  Shot on like the arrow's whirr,
Till the hand no longer could hold the rein,
  Nor the heel could plunge the spur;
His limbs all droop'd like a dead man's limbs,
  But his steed did not pause at all:
Away, away! was the rider whirled—
  'T was wondrous he did not fall!
His finger was girt by a little ring!
  He look'd upon it by chance,

And, with a cry you might hear afar,
He sprang from his drowsy trance;
He seized the reins—from his courser's flanks
Hot blood o'er the rowels splash'd;
"Away! away!" he shouted aloud,
And away, and away, he dash'd.
Away, and away, for many an hour,
He darted, for many a mile;
The courser smok'd as all on a flame,
And the blood in his veins did boil.
Away, away! still he dashes on,
As a sinner would fly from death,
Till the courser's bounds grew less and less,
And he labors to heave a breath;
"Away! away!" still the cavalier cried,
Still spurring the coal-black steed;
But the shout too faint, and the gore-clogg'd spurs,
Too blunt to provoke his speed.
Yet onward he toil'd, till a broad deep stream
On a sudden check'd the path:
The cavalier sprung from the steed to the ground,
And he stamp'd on the ground in wrath;
He stamp'd on the ground, and he beat his brow,—
One glance at the ring he cast:
Oh! then might it seem o'er his features fierce
The scowl of a demon past!
Again on his coal-black steed he sprung,
And never a word he said,

But the sweat from his courser's mane he wrung,
And patted his bending head;
The courser neigh'd—with a sudden bound
His rider through air he bore:
He shot to the other side of the stream,
Then fell to arise no more.

## PART SECOND.

The little blades of the tender grass
The ground in soft verdure hide,
And the leafy boughs of clustering trees
Are nodding on every side;
And on every bough of every tree
The birds in bright plumage glance,
While to the beat of their tiny feet,
The leaves all around them dance,
And every bird doth most sweetly sing,
And right blithsome is their song,
And the breeze attempers its voice with theirs,
As softly it steals along;
But a sweeter sound than the song of bird,
Or the murmur of passing air—
Oh! a sweeter song by far may be heard—
'T is the voice of a lady fair.
That lady is fair as lady may be,
Too fair for this world of ours;

As a blessed vision she might appear,
  Come down from the heavenly bowers.
A young boy near her, holds by the rein
  A palfrey as white as snow,
For never a speck of other hue
  On a hair of his can you show.
His mane is long as a lion's mane,
  His tail to the ground is rolled;
And he is bedight in caparisons rich,
  All gemmed with silver and gold.
The lady signs, and the little page hastes
  With the palfrey to her side;
She lays her hand on the palfrey's neck,
  As if she would mount and ride;
But there is a rustle among the leaves—
  She pauses to know whence it be,
And a man comes forth, and reels to her feet,
  And kneels him down on his knee—
He kneels him down on his knee, and signs
  The sign of the cross on his breast,
While the lady scanneth his form and face,
  And the garb in which he is drest.
His form seems faint as a helpless babe's,
  Yet in sooth 't is a noble one;
His face drops sweat, as the sky drops rain,
  And is red as the setting sun.
His garb is rich, but in many a place
  Is rent, as in furious toil;

He is booted and spurred as should cavalier be,
  And his heels have a bloody soil.
The stranger's bosom heaveth amain,
  As he kneels to the damsel fair;
His lips are too parch'd to shape a word,
  And he hath not a breath to spare.
"O stranger, what art thou? and why art thou here?
  And why dost thou kneel on thy knee?
Arise from thy knee, and stand on thy feet,
  And tell me what wouldst thou with me?"
Again the stranger essay'd to speak,
  But essay'd to speak in vain,
For his lips were parched as the lips of death,
  And his breath still heaved amain:
He sprang to his feet, he stamped on the ground,
  And his teeth in fury gnashed,
And he bit his lip till the blood trickled down,
  And his eyes like a demon's flashed:
And he laid his hand on the palfrey white,
  As if upon it to spring;
The lady's eye to his finger he turned,
  Which was girt with a little ring;
He pointed then to the bloody spurs,
  And then to a distant way,
And then again to the palfrey white,
  But never a word could he say.
"Beshrew thy meaning," the lady said,
  "Art thou such an ungallant knight,

A lady must tread on a weary foot,
  While thou ridest her palfrey white?"
He put his hand to his girdle then,
  And a heavy purse he drew,
And that heavy purse all filled with gold,
  To the lady's page he threw;
And a golden chain, with a diamond bright,
  He tore from his breast in haste,
And that chain of gold, and that jewel rich,
  In the lady's hand he placed.
Then to the palfrey he turned again;
  But his arm the lady caught:
"Nay, keep thy jewels, and keep thy gold,
  The palfrey is thine unbought;
And I would for thy sake, thou weary knight,
  I could give thee a braver steed;
But here thou must take thy rest awhile,
  For rest thou surely dost need."
No word he said, but he shook his head,
  And again he pointed away;
But she held him the faster by the arm—
  "Now thou shalt not say me nay!"
She looked in his face with her eyes so blue,
  So beautiful, and so soft,
And the stranger felt his dark eyes melt,
  As they had not melted oft.
A light breeze played, and her coal-black curls
  Were wafted against his cheek,

And the delicate touch thrilled his every vein,
 And rendered his purpose weak;
But when she leaned her head, and he felt
 Her cheek imparting its glow
To his own, and her breath to blend with his
 Was sent in a rosy flow,
What wonder that by her charms, such sway
 In that moment was o'er him won,
That could he have spoken, he could but say,
 "Sweet lady, thy will be done!"
Upon a soft bed of thornless flowers,
 The lady bade him recline,
And the little page went at her sign, and brought
 In each hand a goblet of wine.
"Now pledge me, sir knight," said the lady fair,
 And he raised the brim to his lip;
But he suddenly dashed his cup to the ground,
 As hers she began to sip;
For the little ring which his finger girt,
 Again attracted his eye,
And he started up from the bed of flowers,
 With a loud and fearful cry;
She seized his arm, he flung her away—
 He sprung on the palfrey white,
And, like the lightning's vanishing flash,
 He shot from the lady's sight.

## PART THIRD.

The moon is throned in the lovely blue,
  Which melting upon the eye,
Allures the wish to be ushered there,
  Reclined in its depths to lie·
As yet one visible star alone
  The azure realm divides,
Which burns with a bright, though trembling light,
  As before its queen it glides;
On the dew-gemm'd leaves, on the placid waves,
  The showering moon-beams play—
A beauty floats o'er all earth and sky,
  That would shame the glory of day.
But there cannot be a thing of life
  Beholding this lovely scene,
Or its very breath could now be heard
  Disturbing the silence serene.
But see; yon river, so calm till now,
  Is stirred, but not by the gale;
And gliding slowly towards the shore
  Some object appears to sail;
But what can it be? to the distant eye,
  Which a glance upon it would throw,
'T would seem the image of yon pale cloud,
  Or a drifting heap of snow.

It sinks, it rises, it floats along
  Till upon the shore 't is thrown,
And there it lies, as immovable
  As a thing to life unknown.
Now all is calm, till from yonder wood
  A cavalier suddenly starts,
On a steed, which despite his voice and rein,
  Right on to the river darts;
But he suddenly paused as motionless,
  As he had no power to stir,
Nor even to breathe, nor seemed he to feel
  The plunge of his rider's spur.
The cavalier thought he heard a sigh;
  He eagerly looked around;
On a human form he cast his eye
  He hastily sprung to the ground:
He raised the form, and he threw aside
  The folds of the snow-white veil,
And the moonlight flowed, in a silver tide,
  On features lovely and pale.
The cavalier starting dropped the form,
  As the features met his sight,
'Twas the very lady from whom, but now,
  He had taken the palfrey white;
But again he raised her in his arms,
  And he laid her upon his breast;
He wrung the brine from her coal-black hair
  And his lips to hers he prest

There was no warmth, nor a sign of life,
  But upon those lips alone;
And perhaps the warmth those lips bestowed,
  They but received from his own.
In vain he sought to recall her to life;
  So, that some aid he might find,
Upon the palfrey he laid her form,
  And he mounted himself behind.
The steed, which had almost breathless stood,
  Neigh'd with a terrible sound:
With the knight and the lady into the waves
  He dash'd, with a headlong bound.
The cavalier's efforts little avail'd
  The maid or himself to sustain—
The waves closed o'er him, and gushed in his ears,
  And whirled his bewildered brain.
He raised his head, and opened his eye,
  How strange was the scene he met:
He lay in a lordly hall unharm'd,
  Nor one spot of his robe was wet,
In the midst of the hall he saw a throne,
  With a sceptre and diadem;
A lady entered, shrined in a veil,
  Which burn'd with many a gem—
She took the cavalier by the hand,
  And aside she flung her veil;
Fair as the blush of morn was the cheek,
  Which late he had seen so pale;

And her raven ringlets down her neck
  In wild luxuriance danced,
And her eyes—her sweet blue eyes—on his
  In melting tenderness glanced.
She led him toward the throne, and sign'd
  As there he should take his seat;
But he waved his hand, and shook his head,
  And kneel'd him down at her feet;
And as he knelt, emotions he felt
  Which were far too sweet to speak;
Till, glancing his eye toward his hand,
  He started up with a shriek:
"Lady, lady, detain me not!
  For a deed is to be done;
In beauty's cause must this sword be drawn
  By the dawn of to-morrow's sun!"
"In beauty's cause? I fear me, sir knight,
  For beauty small is thy care;
And little, methinks, thy courtesy,
  If thou wilt not hear my prayer.
Now hear me, sir knight, by royal birthright
  A wide dominion I sway,
But a bold usurper has risen in might,
  To make my kingdom his prey.
Sir knight, I am a defenceless maid,
  And well I may wish to call
A knight so noble and brave as thou,
  Friend, champion, lover, and all!

Yes, *lover*, sir knight, for wouldst thou but stay
  Till to-morrow, and meet my foe,
My heart, my hand, my kingdom, my all,
  As thy guerdon would I bestow!"
She threw her white arms around his knees,
  As she knelt at the cavalier's feet;
And she looked in his face—he could ill resist
  That look so imploring and sweet!
But he cast one glance upon his ring,
  And her clasp he then unbound;
And he said—but with a faltering voice—
  As he raised her from the ground—
"This moment I must hasten away,
  In the cause of my lady love;
But when her rescue shall be achieved,
  So bless me the saints above,
As I shall retnrn, with all speed I may,
  This arm to devote for thee;
I swear me thy friend and thy champion,
  Though thy lover I may not be!"
"One moment, sir knight, let me know the claim
  Of her who calls thee away;
If that claim is just, I will pardon thee,
  "Nor longer demand thy stay."
The knight was impatient to be gone,
  But was check'd by her tender hold,
And he had not the heart to spurn her off,
  So briefly his tale he told.

## PART FOURTH.

### THE CAVALIER'S TALE.

I LOVED, and was belov'd the same:
Her young heart had not learn'd
The world's dissembling forms; her flame
Pure and unhidden burned:
But noticed by her father's eye,
It soon alarmed his pride:
For his were birth and grandeur high,
Which fate to me denied.
Compelled to part, with broken heart,
I rush'd the war to seek;
But first we both exchanged an oath,
The dearest love could speak.
The ring, which girds my finger now,
I bade her cherish ever,
As a memorial of our vow,
To love and love forever.
I sought the field, I forced to yield
Full many a Paynim foe;
Methinks her prayers have been my shield:
No arm could lay me low.
And now I had returned in fame
My native land to hail,
When there a page to meet me came,
Who told a fearful tale;

The every word convulsed my frame,
My cheek turned ashy pale.
He told me that my true-love dear
Was left an orphan maid,
Beneath a guardian's care severe,
Who dared her rights invade;
Who with usurping grasp detained
Her father's gold and land;
Nor his presumption there restrained,
But dared to claim her hand;
And e'en had sworn, if by her scorn
His suit were still denied,
Upon the third return of morn
Should ruder means be tried.
To-morrow is the destin'd day,
But we ere then shall meet:
I trust this arm the wretch shall lay
Before my lady's feet.
To shield her from his brutal rage,
The arm of love to bring,
She sent in haste her faithful page,
To seek me with this ring—
The ring, which when our vows were made,
I on her finger placed:
But, lady, I'm too long delay'd—
To save her I must haste!
But for her sake, thou lady bright,
My heart would own thy spell;

But for her sake I could not slight
  Thy charms angelical;
But for her sake, not thus I might,
  Have power to say, farewell!

## PART FIFTH.

One moment the cavalier waits reply,
  On his ear no answer falls;
He looks around, and amazed he stands
  By his lady's castle walls.
He looked around, but he looked in vain
  For the lovely stranger-queen;
Again his gaze he fixed in amaze,
  On the unexpected scene;
And as he looked on the well-known towers,
  On his mind recollections rushed
Of his childhood bliss, and his boyhood love,
  Till the tears unbidden gushed:
But he swept the glimmering from his eye,
  And looking to heaven he said,
"Saint Mary be thank'd, by whatever means
  So sudden the space has fled,
Which parted me from my lady's foe;
  Saint Mary, arm me this morn!"
His sword clash'd on the vibrating shield,
  And loudly he blew the horn.

Every portal expanded wide,
  But he saw no mortal near;
Onward he strode from hall to hall,
  But he found no foe appear.
Onward he strode, till checked by a gate,
  Which was locked and barred as yet;
As it yielded to his gauntlet's stroke.
  A throng he suddenly met;
They rushed upon him, he knew not whence;
  But from their rude grasp he sprung
With such violent force, that by the shock
  They all to the ground were flung.
Again they rose, and on every side
  Their weapons the knight assailed.
He fought full well, and he fought full long,
  But at last his foes prevailed:
Still, though by their numbers overpowered,
  He struggled as best he could,
Till the ring from his finger dropped to earth,
  And all in amazement stood;
For the ring, expanding, girt the hall
  In a circle of burning flame,
And contracting, around the cavalier's foes,
  Nearer and nearer it came,
Till all were wither'd in its embrace,
  But harmless it pass'd the knight:
In a moment, the ring, and a heap of dust,
  Alone remain'd to his sight.

The ring on his finger he replaced,
  And he found his strength regained
That moment; again from hall to hall,
  Uninjured and unrestrained,
He past, till again his onward way
  Was checked by a massy gate;
In vain his efforts to burst the lock,
  Or shake one bar of the grate;
A laugh of derision shook the walls:
  Through the bars he could see appear
A being of lofty size, whose lip
  Was curled with a fiend-like sneer,
As he pointed to a lady pale,
  Who lifeless lay at his feet:
The cavalier struggled with frantic rage,
  Impatient the wretch to meet;
But he raged in vain, till he thought he heard
  The musical whispering
Of a sweet tender voice, which said,
  "Now bethink thee of thy ring!"
Obeying the voice, he instantly
  The ring from his finger drew;
Again expanding, its fiery wreath
  O'er the massy bars it threw:
They dropp'd to the ground like molten lead;
  Onward rushed the eager knight,
But he found not the lady nor his foe,
  Who had borne her from his sight.

The little ring he snatched from the ground
  And on his finger replaced,
He clash'd his shield again and again,
  Till the foe stepped forth in haste;
One scowl they exchanged, but paused not for speech.
  At the clash of each mighty stroke
Their weapons quivered, until at last
  The sword of the cavalier broke;
He flung it aside, he seized his foe,
  As to grapple his life away;
They struggled as every nerve would burst,
  Till sinking together, they
Exhausted upon the ground reclined,
  Yet struggling in vain to rise;
And oft as their glances met, the rage
  Of a demon flashed in their eyes.
Hark! O hark! it seems that all earth
  Upon its foundation rocks,
While ten thousand thunders tear the skies
  In loud and repeated shocks.
The tottering roof, the falling walls,
  The knight and the foe behold;
But each still writhes in the other's arms,
  Which grasp him in desperate fold.
The roof now bursts with an awful crash,
  And before their shuddering eye
Appeared unfolded a sheet of fire,
  Enwrapping all earth and sky!

A shriek was heard—the loftiest tower
  That moment in ruin crashed,
And disclosed a maid, who stood on high,
  Where destruction around her flashed;
Her white robes dishevelled o'er her hung,
  And waved in the blazing air,
Which danced around her shuddering limbs,
  And wreath'd in her raven hair.
The cavalier would have rushed to her aid,
  But he could not burst the grasp
Of his foe, which so closely pressed him now,
  That he scarce had power to gasp.
The cavalier raged at the savage grin,
  And the glance of malicious scorn;
But the more his rage, the more the mirth
  On the hated features worn.
"Now by this ring," said the cavalier,
  "If near me be any power
Propitious to faithful love like mine,
  Its favor I claim this hour."
Instantly in a whirlwind of flame
  The ground was asunder rent,
And shrieking down the burning abyss
  His foe from his sight was sent.
The knight look'd up where the lady stood;
  A tower trembled o'er her head;
The scorching flame and the smothering smoke,
  More thickly around her spread;

The ruins rolled from his climbing foot,
As he rush'd through the smoke and blaze:
In a moment the lady sunk in his arms,
Shrieking with fear and amaze.
He looks below, but the awful depth
Forbids the desperate spring.
Nor can he on the ruins descend,
While his arms to the lady cling.
He looks above, O merciful heaven!
The tower now bends to its fall!
The knight in despair, could scarce breathe a prayer,
On the guardian power to call.
He heard a crash—he averted his eye—
Nearer he drew to his breast
The lady, as he said, "We must die,
But dying with thee I am blest!"

## PART SIXTH.

The knight looked around—he could ill expect
Such a scene would his eye await:
Unharmed the lady lay at his feet,
By his father's castle-gate.
The vassals clasped his knees, and his name
Repeated in shouts of joy;
And forth the old warrior tottering came
To welcome his gallant boy.

As soon as the cavalier was released
  From the fond paternal embrace,
He raised the lady, who lay at his feet,
  And eagerly looked in her face;
He started away, he clenched his hands,
  He gnashed his teeth in despair;
" Is it thou I have saved from those fatal towers—
  While *she*—has she perish'd there ? "
She opened her eyes, she sprung to his neck—
  " My love, and art thou restored ?
The dangers I 've met, I shall not regret,
  Since redeemed by my true-love's sword."
Such voice, such look, he had heard and seen
  In the joy of his youthful day;
But the features are those of the stranger-queen,
  Who tempted him on his way.
He looks again, and he cannot tell
  If it be his true-love or not;
For, perhaps in his absence, some trait of hers
  Might either be changed or forgot.
Raising his eye, he saw on the sky
  A halo of dazzling light,
And in a car, with many a star,
  Bespangled, a being bright
Was seen to glide, till it paused beside
  The wondering lady and knight.
From her dazzling face, when it hover'd near,
  They hid their eyes on the ground:

Her accents floated into their ear,
  In soft and musical sound:
"Arise, sir knight, she bids thee arise,
  Who has well approved thy worth;
Arise, fair maid, she bids thee arise,
  Who has loved thee from thy birth.
Nay, lady, shun not my presence thus,
  As it threatened danger nigh;
Thy dearest welcome I should command,
  Thy Guardian Genius am I.
From thy earliest hour it has been my care
  To shield thee from every ill,
And my guardian wing shall o'ershadow thee
  To thy latest moment still.
Sir knight, 't was I who the token brought
  To tell thee thy lady's need;
'T was I who wing'd thy impetuous flight
  Upon an unearthly steed;
'T was I who assumed this lady's charms,
  The fairest that can be worn,
Surpassing all by thy memory sketch'd
  Of the dawn of her beauty's morn;
And thus I met thee in beauty's bower,
  And in regal grandeur's hall,
Where the smile of love, nor ambition's power,
  Thy heart could change or inthrall.
Through many perils hast thou been led,
  But thy soul its strength approved;

Many temptations around thee spread,
  But thy faith was still unmoved.
Thine is a heart that can never be
  Estranged from constancy's reign,
And to such a heart the hand is due
  Which else thou shouldst ne'er obtain.
Here is the ring, restore it, sir knight,
  To the hand I now link to thine;
Of your heart's dearest oath, let it be to you both
  For ever and ever the sign.
The ring was to thee a talisman
  To save thee all danger through;
This ring on thy hand, and truth in thy soul,
  No evil could thee subdue.
And should the spell from the ring depart,
  When danger again is known,
Little the need of thy faithful heart
  For other aid than its own.
Ye faithful pair, it shall be my care
  That blessings shall both await;
But if at times ye are doomed to bear
  The scowl of a darker fate,
Ye still may triumph o'er its control,
  If ye still to each other cling;
For evil can never enslave the soul
  Encircled by CONSTANCY'S RING.

# THE SPIRIT OF VENGEANCE.

## A DRAMA.

### IN THREE ACTS.

---

Who sins against another
Sins most against himself.

## DRAMATIS PERSONÆ.

The Stranger.

Count Ernaldo.

Reginald.

The Prince.

Manuel.

Theresa.

Isabelle.

Julia.

---

Scene—*Spain.* Time—*Twenty-four Hours.*

# THE SPIRIT OF VENGEANCE.

## ACT I.

SCENE 1.—*A neglected path, leading to the ruins of a castle.*

*Enter* THERESA *with* MANUEL *approaching the ruins.*

THERESA. Lean on my arm.
MANUEL. Nay! I can go no further.
Here let us rest a moment.
[*Throwing himself languidly upon the ground.*
THERESA. Sweetest rest
Descend upon thee!—never mayst thou know
The weariness of heart. [*Advancing to the ruins.*
Ah! *here* indeed
Should be our resting-place. But all is changed!
Are these my halls of pride? is this my home
Of joy? the home of desolation now
And ruin; here the sole inhabitants,
As in my bosom! Hail! ye fallen towers!

Hail! image of my fortunes! in your look
Is silent sympathy! A thousand welcomes—
If ye could but restore him, at whose side
Smiling I last approached you, never more
To smile again;—but ye are now no place
For him, who as my jealous ear informed me,
Resuming rank and fortune, glads his pride,
Forgetting the forsaken. Yet once more,
Ye cherished halls, will I traverse the scenes
Of happiness departed. Come, my child,
To thy inheritance!

MANUEL. [*Starting up as if from sleep.*] What says my mother?

THERESA. These ruins may afford a safer shelter
To thy repose.

MANUEL. Watched by a mother's eye
Is safety everywhere. [*Exeunt.*

SCENE 2.—*A room in the castle rudely fitted up as a hermitage; a dim lamp on the table. The background is in complete darkness.*

*Enter* THERESA *and* MANUEL.

THERESA. At last we have tracked the light; but even here
Is desolation's home, or—Heaven forbid—
Perhaps the den of guilt.

MANUEL. Guilt dwells not here:—
Behold that type of heaven!

[*Pointing to a crucifix on the table.*

THERESA. Some anchorite
Has centered here his world. Would he were present;
But surely he will pardon to a mother
The liberty her child's relief compels.
Here, rest thee on this pallet.

MANUEL. I will pray first
As at my own dear home,—would we were there:—
My Heavenly Father! bless my dearest mother,
And bless my earthly father and restore him
To her and me.

[*A dark figure emerges from the gloom, glides to the child, and exclaims,* Rise!

THERESA. Heaven defend my child!

STRANGER. Is that thy mother, boy?

MANUEL. Yes—do not harm her.

STRANGER. Didst thou not call upon her, and thy father,
*His* blessing whom I must not name?

MANUEL. His blessing
Abide upon us all.

STRANGER. A goodly jest!
Hell hears and shouts derision! What! His blessing
On *me!*—Perdition! that a foolish babe
Should mock me thus!

THERESA. Mercy, thou terrible man!

STRANGER. Man!

THERESA. Awful being, whatsoe'er thou art,
Give me my child, and let us go in peace.
STRANGER. And where is peace?—No matter,—'t is no place
For me. Come hither, boy.
MANUEL. Oh! save me, mother,
His eyes are burning fire!
STRANGER. Thou dost not know
The evil from the good, or thou wouldst cling
To me, not her. She save thee? I can save thee
From many a curse that she may else be thanked for.
Fool! never bless thy parents,—they of all
Have cursed thee most;—thou hast not words to answer
Their curse, but I will help thee. Come, I 'll teach thee
A proper orison.
THERESA. We must not hear
Such words. Come, we must hence.
STRANGER. Thou trembling fool,
What power can bear you hence against my will?
Stir, if you can.
THERESA. Be thou of earth or hell!
STRANGER. Say that thou fearest me not.
THERESA. I cannot say it,
For terrible thou art. Yet in my soul
Is something holy that should awe thee,—yes,
Shall awe thee.
STRANGER. Name this wonder, and if heaven
And earth shake at the sound—I—I shall smile.

THERESA. A mother's love!
STRANGER. A fable, a fair word,
Repeated for the beauty of its music,
And not its truth. There never was a mother,
Howe'er she romanced of a mother's love,
Would do the only deed that should express it.
THERESA. I would—Heaven knows I would!
STRANGER. But I know better.
How beautiful thy child—how sweet his face
Of eloquent persuasion! purity
His brow has moulded of the snows of heaven,
Which even affection, with her lips of fire,
Trembles to touch, lest it should melt.
THERESA. Thy voice
Is music now.
STRANGER. A spirit not of earth,
Insphered in the dark beauty of his eyes,
Beams glorious as the angel in the sun.
THERESA. Say on—my ear will never tire.
STRANGER. [*Catching* MANUEL *in his arms.*] Fair boy—
Nay, struggle not—I have no will to harm thee.
Little my kindness to the sons of men,
Yet there is something in thy innocent face
Sways me beyond my wont. I'll render thee
The best of blessings, better, better far
Than parents ever give.
THERESA. And that is—
STRANGER. Death! [*Aiming a dagger at the child.*

THERESA. Death! Shield us heavenly Father! spare, oh spare him!
Kill *me*—I care not—but my child! my child!
Let him but live, and I will kiss the dagger
That drinks my life-blood.

MANUEL. I will die first, mother!

STRANGER. Behold a mother's love! Thou bidst him live?

THERESA. Oh yes!

STRANGER. So be it then; and I disclaim
The moment's mercy that was as a ripple
On ocean's stilled infinitude; all sinks
Again to a stern deadness. Far from me
Be it to snatch a mortal from the curse
Of life.

THERESA. My child, my love, again I have thee!

STRANGER. Now for a parent's part.

[*Snatching the boy again.*

THERESA. Forbear! forbear!
Wouldst thou recall thy mercy?

STRANGER. 'T was recalled
When I forbore to strike. Thou bidst him live—
Well, so do I,—but if it be in love
Better by far were hate. Live, boy, yes, live!
But to what end? To forfeit innocence,
The sunlight of thy soul, which thou must bury
In darkness, crushing darkness! Live! for what?

To have the roses of thy young affections
Devoured by adders, gnawing through thy heart
A path for desolation.—Live! for what?
To toil, to weep, to groan,—to kiss the rod
Thou canst not fly nor brave, and scarce canst bear;
To find in all that by the name of joy
Provokes thy toilsome chase, a tiresome curse
That better had been fled—the milk of kindness
Turn into gall and bitterness—abhor
All that surrounds thee!—and thyself the most!
Live—wish for death—yet live, and dare not die,
Held back by coward conscience. Live for this!
'T is all that mortals live for!

MANUEL. Better die!

THERESA. And leave thy mother?

MANUEL. No—for thy dear sake
Alike to me were welcome life or death.

STRANGER. I tell thee, woman, thou art most unworthy
The fondness of this fool, or thou wouldst rather
Guide than withhold my arm against his life—
For were he now to die, canst thou believe
But that his sinless spirit, bursting forth
On cherub wings, would rush to the abode
Of bliss eternal, which, continuing here,
He may forever forfeit?

THERESA. God of mercy!
Save me from madness! close my ear against
Such horrible suggestions.

STRANGER. Mark me, woman!
Be what I may, I once have been a child,
As innocent and blest as now is thine,
As near as he to heaven. What am I now!—
Oh then why died I not!—why came not then
Some pitying angel, from a world to snatch me
Where only guilt and horror lay before me!—
Why dost thou weep?

MANUEL. For thee!

[*The* STRANGER *turns away in deep agitation.*

THERESA. Oh may those tears,
Like dews of heaven descending on his heart,
Melt it to penitence that heralds peace!

MANUEL. Poor man, we 'll pray for thee.

STRANGER. The angelic host
Might kneel in vain—the eternal doom is fixed—
So be it—I will bear.—But thou, sweet boy,
Thou who hast wept for me who never claimed
A tear,—I must reward thee. [*Offering to stab him.*

THERESA. Help! oh God!
Mercy—my child—oh spare him!

[REGINALD *enters with his sword drawn, snatches the child, and restores him to* THERESA.

REGINALD. Hither turn
Thy weapon—but perhaps thy coward arm
Copes but with babes and women.

STRANGER. Calm thee, youth;
My war is with the soul.

MANUEL. [*To* REGINALD.] Nay, gentle sir,
We pray thee harm him not.

THERESA. We but implore thee
To bear us hence in safety.

REGINALD. We again
Must meet. I 'll find thee here?

STRANGER. I shall be found
Where least thou canst expect.—It may be, child,
*We* shall not meet again. Thou wilt remember
This hour, and glory in thy moment's power
To soften adamant; but pray forget not
It was but for a moment. I am now
Myself again, and hating thee, as all
Mankind, I say alike to them and thee—
Live, and my curse upon you!

THERESA. Let us fly!

REGINALD. Lady, where wouldst thou go?

THERESA. To Count Ernaldo.

REGINALD. [*Starting.*] Ernaldo!

STRANGER. Hell! Ernaldo!—let me see—
It is—I did not think another drop
Could fall on my black ocean—yes, that face
Though changed, is not forgotten. Didst thou say
Ernaldo? Tell me what thou art to him?

THERESA. His wife.

STRANGER. And this?

THERESA. His child.

STRANGER. And I have cursed him

REGINALD. I know Ernaldo well, the best of men;
His wife has long been dead.

THERESA. Alas, thy words
Confirm my fears; I have been so forgotten
That he could wed another.

STRANGER. Didst thou call him
The best of men? I 've done him much injustice
If he deserves that name.

REGINALD. He well deserves it,
For by him, though a stranger to his blood,
Have I been reared from earliest infancy
With all a father's care.

STRANGER. Hadst thou no claim
Upon it?

REGINALD. None.

STRANGER. Thy kindred?

REGINALD. They have never
Been known to him.

STRANGER. Nor thee?

REGINALD. Thou hast no right
To question me.

STRANGER. A stranger—even his kindred
Unknown—Ernaldo generous—I know better—
Those lineaments, and even that voice—t 'is so—
It *must* be so—yet what shall that avail me—
Oh glorious thought! the heaven of my revenge
Opens at last before me!

REGINALD. With your pleasure,

Lady, 't were best to go. These are but ravings
Not worth our hearing. Come.

STRANGER. Against my will
You cannot.

REGINALD. That 's to prove.

STRANGER. One moment, lady,
Then, if thou wilt, depart.

[*He discovers his face to* THERESA, *who shrieks and falls insensible.*

REGINALD. What hast thou done?

MANUEL. My mother! oh, my mother!

REGINALD. Hush! she lives.

THERESA. Where is he?

STRANGER. Here, Theresa. Nay, be calm.
Breathe not my name, not even to thy child.
My friend, excuse the hint, but we can spare
Your further company.

THERESA. Kind sir, forgive
The trouble we have given you. Leave us with him.

MANUEL. But mother, art thou safe?

STRANGER. Before we part,
I charge thee never to inform Ernaldo
What thou hast witnessed.

REGINALD. Why should his wife and child
Be kept from him?

STRANGER. *His* wife and child?—Ah, yes!
Thou speakest of *these?* Far be it from my purpose!
I shall myself at the expedient time

Conduct them to him, and that time is near,
Nearer than he may wish; till then I claim
Thy silence.

REGINALD. Lady?

THERESA. Yes, I supplicate thee
Do all that he requires.

REGINALD. Well, for thy sake—— [*Exit.*

THERESA. [*After a pause.*] And is it thus—

STRANGER. Be silent. Go before me.

MANUEL. Not to that place of darkness.

STRANGER. Canst thou fear?

MANUEL. I fear but for my mother.

THERESA. [*As they retire and disappear in the darkness.*] No, my child,
Fear nothing: we are safe.

[*The* STRANGER *bursts into a terrible laugh;* THERESA *shrieks. Scene changes.*

SCENE 3.—*A hall in the palace of* COUNT ERNALDO. *Enter* ERNALDO *and* ISABELLE.

ERNALDO. The time has come, my daughter, to unfold
The dearest purpose of my secret soul,
Which should have been discovered long before,
But that I dread thy answer.

ISABELLE. Am I not
Thy child, whose duty is to do thy will?
Or am I of the weak and selfish nature

That ever shrinks from duty?
ERNALDO. I acknowledge
Never had father child more dutiful
And excellent, yet for that very cause
I dare not name the wish that *must* be granted:
For should it prove unwelcome——
ISABELLE. There is nothing
Unwelcome to me in the way of duty.
I have observed at times that something weighs
Upon thy mind; I should be proud, my father,
If destined to remove it.
ERNALDO. So thou art.
ISABELLE. And how?
ERNALDO. I know thee prudent, I am sure;
Thou hast not acted like those silly girls,
Who plight their hearts and hands without the knowledge
Of those who gave them life.
ISABELLE. It does not please me
To be suspected.
ERNALDO. Nor do I suspect thee;
No, I am confident thy hand and heart
Are free, or I should know it——
ISABELLE. But my father——
ERNALDO. What are thy thoughts of Reginald?
ISABELLE. The question
Is strange.
ERNALDO. But needs an answer.
ISABELLE. I suppose him

Conscious of what he owes, and duly grateful.

ERNALDO. A noble youth, is it not?

ISABELLE. It is not likely
He should be so in birth, and for his spirit,
As yet it is not proved.

ERNALDO. Thou art deceived;
He is of noble bearing, and his birth——

ISABELLE. It is unknown to all.

ERNALDO. True—very true—
Yet how can it be base? Sure his demeanor
Forbids such thought.

ISABELLE. I think it would be easy
To find a worthier theme.

ERNALDO. Then Reginald
Is one thou dost not like?

ISABELLE. I neither care to like
Or to dislike him, more than others
Of our domestics.

ERNALDO. Our domestics, child?
I shall be angry; never dare apply
That name to Reginald.

ISABELLE. I have no will
To speak or hear of him.

ERNALDO. And when thou dost,
Be it as he were my son.

ISABELLE. Heavens! how I scorn
Thus to degrade my father!

ERNALDO. Yes, *my son.*

And such of right he shall become by thee;
He loves thee well——

ISABELLE. How! the audacious slave!
And dares he——

ERNALDO. Never is his passion breathed
In words, but it hath visible utterance
In all his looks and actions.

ISABELLE. Is it thus
That he repays thee? Make him know himself,
And turn him forth, the outcast that he was,
Before thy bounty gave the daily bread
And nightly shelter he so ill deserves.

ERNALDO. Thou art the least deserving of the two,
Thou disobedient girl!—Stir not my anger,
Or tremble! for by heaven I 'll cast thee forth
From the paternal door, to meet the fate
Thou willest his, and care not shouldst thou sink
In guilt and infamy.

ISABELLE. Let the worst come,
Guilt or dishonor never can approach me,
The not unworthy scion of a house
They never have polluted.

ERNALDO. [*With vehemence.*] Would to God!——

ISABELLE. Sir?

ERNALDO. I forget, speak we of Reginald.
He must be thine; if willingly received,
The better—with him be my blessing thine;
But shouldst thou still rebel—woe on thy head!

Thine be thy father's curse, and none the less
My will shall be obeyed.

ISABELLE. No curse less welcome
Than Reginald. Ernaldo! what! a child
Of thy illustrious house, and link myself
To him, some peasant's brat! the shame were worse
Than death a thousand times!

ERNALDO. Thou speakest this
In ignorance; but I am too indulgent
To parley thus. I should employ the rights
That fathers claim from Heaven.

ISABELLE. Have they a right
To make their children wretched?

ERNALDO. Say no more,
For my resolve is fixed.

ISABELLE. And so is mine.
Unbidden I shall fly the house, exposed
To poverty, to death, I care not what,
But Reginald shall never call me his.
Now let thy anger work.

ERNALDO. [*After a moment's thoughtfulness.*] It shall not yet:
I will not go to the extremity
Till other means all fail. I have been harsh
Beyond my wont, but I am tasked to this
By fate imperative.—My child, no peace
Can ever enter in thy father's mind,
No joy on earth, or hope of joy in heaven,

Till thou dost grant me this.
ISABELLE. I am amazed!
Let me but know how this may be—
ERNALDO. I dare not.
ISABELLE. I yield not then to artful supplications
More than to savage threats.
ERNALDO. [*Kneeling.*] Could I abase me
To this in artifice?—Behold, I kneel—
Thy father kneels, thy father calls upon thee
To save him—save him from the hell within him,
And that which yawns beneath him!
ISABELLE. And all this
By being Reginald's?
ERNALDO. Oh yes!
ISABELLE. I marvel
Why thou shouldst be so earnest in an object
That offers nothing visible, except
Dishonor to our house. If thou art swayed
By reason and by honor, give me proof,
And I submit. Why shouldst thou hide thy motives
Unless dishonorable? and if so,
That attitude becomes thee, and is one
I would not bid thee change, yet have no pleasure
To see my father in. Excuse me, sir. [*Exit.*
ERNALDO. And so the only means of reparation
Is thrust beyond my reach! Am I to blame;
Who placed that means beyond me?—not myself;
Witness how diligently I pursued it,

How low I cast myself,—and all in vain!
What other means appears? There yet is one,
But to accomplish this I must expose me
To every slave's contempt, must die in shame,
The gazing-stock of fools, bequeath my children
My infamy, their sole inheritance,
And cast them naked, houseless, friendless, breadless,
To perish in the pitiless world. Can Heaven
Command me this?

*Enter* REGINALD.

ERNALDO. How sir! it is not well
To burst upon my privacy.

REGINALD. My lord——

ERNALDO. But let that pass, for in a welcome hour
Thou comest; I but now had need of thee
To speak of earnest matters.

REGINALD. To that end
I came, my lord.

ERNALDO. Dost thou anticipate
My question?

REGINALD. No, my lord; be what it may,
My mind will be unfit to ponder on it
Till thou hast answered mine.

ERNALDO. [*Throwing himself carelessly into a seat.*]
I 'm all attention.

REGINALD. Thy part to me, my lord, was ever one

The best of fathers well might imitate,
And gratitude has throned thee in my heart
A very idol there.

Ernaldo. So thou hast need
Of added favors? but the way thou talkest
Is much amiss. Seek not to wind about me
By harping on the past, but let thy wish
Be frankly named, it shall be frankly granted

Reginald. How startled, how indignant, and how anxious,
Is the idolater, when told the thing
His fancy made a god, is but a reptile
Ignoble and detestable! In pity
Redeem me from such doubts, and prove thou art not
Unworthy of my homage!

Ernaldo. [*Starting up trembling with fury.*] Wretch! what devil
Hath sent thee for my torture—speak—by Heaven—
By hell—thou wilt not—speak—or I will tear thee,
Yes, villain! I will tear thee limb from limb,
And fling the mangled fragments to the whirlwinds—
Speak!—who hath told thee this?

Reginald. [*Who has gazed upon him with astonishment and horror, sinks against a pillar, exclaiming in acute anguish.*] I have not erred then!

Ernaldo. Betrayed at last—and death—and shame!—but no—
It cannot be!—'t is false!—curse on thy look

Of doubt—'t is false, I tell thee!—I will swear it—
Yes, I am innocent—look at these hands—
Avaunt, thou grinning fiend!—it is not blood—
It is not blood, I tell thee!—ha! confusion!
One spot escaped! Hell heave thy waves of fire
To cleanse away this stain.

REGINALD. [*Aside.*] My worst of fears
Reached not a crime so horrid; 't is apparent
He sought to slay his wife, and thinks her death
Accomplished. [*As he is retiring,* ERNALDO *rushes to him.*

ERNALDO. Hold, there—stir not on thy life!
Better that thou wert damned than breathe a word
Of this vile lie to others. I repeat
'T is false, and challenge proof.

REGINALD. Oh that I had none!

ERNALDO. None—none—I tell thee none. The only eye
Of witness near, was sealed.

REGINALD. And whose?

ERNALDO. [*Recollecting himself.*] My friend,
I have been mad, and raved I know not what.
Remember not my words. Come, let us speak
Of something near thy interest.

REGINALD. This of all
Is nearest.

ERNALDO. What?

REGINALD. Behold!

*Enter* THERESA *and* MANUEL.

ERNALDO. All hope is over!

REGINALD. Not so. She lives; thou canst repair her wrongs,
And all may yet be well.

ERNALDO. Repair her wrongs!
What power of earth can do it?

REGINALD. Thine, at least
In part.

ERNALDO. Thou canst lay down what terms thou wilt,
For I am in thy power; but I 'm deceived
If thou wilt take ungenerous advantage
Of utter helplessness. Wretch as I am,
That I am not all evil thou hast proof
In what I uncompelled have done for thee.
Thus I implore thee, suppliant at thy feet,
By all that 's noble in thee, spare my life,
And fame, the life of life.

REGINALD. Thy crime, though great,
Is not of those that peril life.

ERNALDO. Thou say it?
Thou speak thus of the wrong that I have done thee?

REGINALD. No wrong have I received from thee, except
That when I see a fellow-creature wronged,
I feel the wrong as mine.

ERNALDO. Either thy soul
Is far beneath a man's or far above it!
Canst *thou* forgive me?—me, who—ah! a thought
Flashes upon me. Lady, hast thou met

This youth before?

[*Awaiting her answer with breathless anxiety.*

THERESA. Yes—once.

ERNALDO. [*Recoils, but recovers himself.*] And when?

THERESA. But now.

ERNALDO. Hope comes again! What knowest thou of this lady? [*To* REGINALD.

REGINALD. That she is thine, and this thy child.

ERNALDO. 'T is well—
'T is excellent! Come, I am merry now,
And I could shout for joy. But thou art sure
She is my wife?

REGINALD. Canst thou deny it?

ERNALDO, Truly
Not I—far be it from my wish.—Thou never
Hast seen her till this day?

REGINALD. Never, my lord.

ERNALDO. Song, dance, and frolic, come! We'll startle earth
With peals of joy! Thy hand, and thine fair wife!
Come hither, little imp. [MANUEL *approaches.*] Come—
Hence! avaunt!
Let me not see that face! 't is *his!*

REGINALD. My lord!

ERNALDO. A sickness comes upon me. Prithee leave me,
I wish to be alone.

REGINALD. Where shall I usher
The lady and her child?

ERNALDO. I care not whither,
So from my sight!

REGINALD. I brought them here, my lord,
To see them righted; and betide what may,
I stir not from them till to that effect
I have thy promise.

ERNALDO. I shall grant the lady
All for herself and child she may desire.
Trouble me not—why linger?—do ye question
My promise? I will swear to it, and as witness
I call on heaven.

THE STRANGER. [*Appearing suddenly.*] Hell comes uncalled!

ERNALDO. Oh God! [*Falls lifeless.*

CURTAIN DROPS.

---

## ACT II.

SCENE 1.—*An apartment in* ERNALDO'S *palace.* ERNALDO *is discovered reclining on a sofa.*

ERNALDO. I laid me down in health, and I awake
In death!—'t is the same place, and yet I know not
How this may be on earth, for it is said
Death sends the spirit hence, and I am dead,
Most surely I am dead—yet is within me

The conscious spirit. Was it all a fable
Of hell and heaven? and doth the spirit still
Abide within the body till dissolved,
And hover o'er it then? 'T is said the souls
Of sinful men are dragged to hell—and I
Have been a fearful sinner—yet where am I?
Perhaps 't was false—ah no! the flames of hell
Arise—they scorch me now—they glow—they burn—
Oh fire!—Is there no hope?—and am I lost
Beyond repeal? I have been told the damned
Can shape no prayer for mercy—Can I pray?—
Father! be merciful! Oh God! oh God!
I 've prayed!—then I am safe!—I may repent
And be forgiven yet!
What! where am I?
Alive, and yet on earth!—'t was but a dream!—
What must those horrors be to the lost wretches
To whom they are no dream!

A Voice. What thine must be!

[Ernaldo, *shuddering, falls on his face. After a moment he slowly raises his head, and looks fearfully around.*

Ernaldo. I was deceived; guilty imagination
Gave audible voice to my tormentor, conscience.
'T was an appalling sound, the very tone
Of him—whom I have silenced—
Am I certain
His spirit is not here?—it is—it is—

Mine cowers before it—oh! an icy thrill
Darts through my shrinking veins—my blood is clotted—
The atmosphere of death is pressed around me,
And human breath forsakes me!
Hark! he comes
Embodied! [*The* PRINCE *enters.*
Yes, I 'll meet thee, for thy look
Will kill, and so release me.

PRINCE. How, my friend!
What hast thou done against me, that my presence
Appals thee?

ERNALDO. Is it thou, my Prince?—but look,
I dare not—look around us—is he gone?
Are we alone?

PRINCE. We are. But may I know
Whose presence awed thee?

ERNALDO. None. I had a dream,
And am but now awakened; but thy presence
My gracious Prince, would banish the remembrance
Of real agonies, so well it may
What but a dream inflicted. Deign accept
My heart's best welcome.

PRINCE. Thanks; I should be happy
To wait on your fair daughter.

ERNALDO. Let me hasten
To announce the honor. [*Exit.*

PRINCE. There 's a courtier for you,
Plotting and smiling. For his daughter's sake,

If possible, I shall not when I crush
His treason, crush him with it.

*Enter* REGINALD.

PRINCE. Gentle youth,
A word.

REGINALD. Your pleasure!

PRINCE. I have well observed
That thou art loved and trusted by Ernaldo
As if thou wert his son.

REGINALD. Sir, these are matters
Concerning but ourselves; and so excuse me
From troubling strangers with them.

PRINCE. Nay, my friend,
I only wished to say the Count's affection
Has fettered thine to him.

REGINALD. It is a question
The Count has never asked, and why should others?

PRINCE. 'T is with no idle notion that I ask it.
It much imports to know if thy affection
Is such to Count Ernaldo, I may trust thee
With my designs to save him from a peril
Inevitable else.

REGINALD. Believe me, then,
At thy command. If peril threats Ernaldo,
All I can do in honor to avert it
I am prepared to do.

PRINCE. Now speak sincerely;
Has he not trusted thee with some design
That he would hide from me?
REGINALD. Dost thou imagine
That I am fit for the participation
Of deeds that shun the light? I can inform thee
Ernaldo thinks not so.
PRINCE. And canst thou swear it?
REGINALD. Thou hast my word, sir; if it is mistrusted,
Does that entitle thee to claim my oath?
But to the point. What the impending danger
To be averted from the Count?
PRINCE. I ask
Thy promise to be silent.
REGINALD. Well, 't is given.
PRINCE. From strongest evidence I have assurance
He is engaged in a disloyal cause,
That must be overthrown before, matured,
It takes the open field, for *then* its fall
Must be Ernaldo's fall; but if in silence
We can defeat its end, he may escape
Unnoticed; for this object it is needful
That thou shouldst wind into his confidence,
And win me added proofs, that when Ernaldo
Confronts them may confound him.
REGINALD. Shame confound me
If e'er I stoop to this! What! I betray
My generous friend! I, who disdain to harm

My deadliest foe, except in open strife!
Hence, else Ernaldo's very roof burst down
To crush his treacherous guest!

PRINCE. Thou peasant slave!
How dares thy touch profane me! [*Flings him off.*

REGINALD. Slave indeed!
[*Drawing his sword.*

*Enter* ERNALDO, *with attendants.*

ERNALDO. Treason!—the Prince!—how, Reginald!—down with him.
Disarm him!—I am truly grieved for this,
My noble Prince; the boy shall answer for it.

REGINALD. And it can well be answered. In thy cause
I did what should be done. This noble Prince
Is here for noble deeds.

PRINCE. I can myself
Unfold them as they are.
[*Signing to the attendants to retire.*
Now, Count Ernaldo,
Reply sincerely, thou shalt not repent it;
Whate'er thy answer, by my princely word
I pledge thy safety. [*Aside.*] He appears disturbed!

ERNALDO. My lord, I cannot think of any question
Whose answer perils me.

PRINCE. And canst thou think
Of what thou art suspected?

ERNALDO. Rot the tongue
That uttered the suspicion!—I am wronged—
'T is false—'t is slanderous—who has dared—away!
[*To* REGINALD.
Fix not that insolent eye in triumph on me!
Hast thou betrayed me?—death!—may furies tear thee!
Yet am I safe—thou hast no proof—my lord,
In all the pride of injured innocence
I stand secure, and smile—

PRINCE. But I have proofs
Unanswerable.

ERNALDO. No—it cannot be—
Think not to start my fears—ha! is it so
Indeed! Then hail the worst—if I must perish
I perish not alone. [*Drawing his sword.*] Impede my way
Who dare — off, villains!

[*He bursts from the attendants, and is rushing away, when the* STRANGER *suddenly appears before him;* ERNALDO *recoils and throws himself into the arms of the attendants.*

ERNALDO. Save me—save me—
Kill me—do what ye will—but save me from him!
Ye lightnings, blast these eyes that fix on his
Despite my will!—Oh save me, Heaven!

STRANGER. Thou fool
What claim hast thou on Heaven?

ERNALDO. Oh that the earth
I grovel on, would burst and swallow me!

STRANGER. Hereafter earth shall render thee that service,
Yea, and a brighter element.

ERNALDO. In mercy
Shield me from his approach.

[*As the* STRANGER *approaches* ERNALDO *he falls convulsed and insensible in the arms of the attendants.*

PRINCE. What art thou?

STRANGER. One, sir
Who loves not yon poor trembler with a love
Passing the love of woman, yet perhaps
About as much. Let that be as it may,
I wish not he should bear another's sins,
Having so many of his own to answer;
He is no traitor to his king.

PRINCE. I cannot
Confide in that assurance.

STRANGER. Follow me:
Thou shalt be satisfied.

[*The* STRANGER *retires: the* PRINCE *follows hesitatingly.*

REGINALD. [*Sustaining* ERNALDO.] How is it with you?

ERNALDO. [*Recovering, looks around bewildered.*
Where are the sulphurous waves? the coiling serpents
Darting their arrowy fire? the laughing fiends
Making a mirth of my calamity?
Methought I was in hell!

REGINALD. Thou art on earth,
And long shalt be, I trust.

ERNALDO. Is it Reginald
Speaks to me? and in kindness? and his arm
Sustains me! Knowest thou what *my* arm has done?
He comes to tell thee—Mercy!

REGINALD. Nay, be calm, sir:
'T is but the Prince.

*The* PRINCE *enters.*

PRINCE. My lord, I am ashamed
Of my unjust suspicions. I believed thee
Conspired against my father's throne, but gladly
I recognize thy innocence.

ERNALDO. If all
His subjects are as loyal as myself
His kingdom has no traitor.

PRINCE. Yet I marvel
What caused thy agitation.

ERNALDO. I had heard
Before of slanderous rumors; and what wonder
It wrung my very soul, to find that even
My Prince could deem me guilty?

PRINCE. I regret it,
But trust thou wilt excuse it, and consent
To knit with me a bond of amity,
The tie, thy daughter's love.

REGINALD. Not Isabelle's?

ERNALDO. Be silent, boy! Most gladly do I welcome
This most unlooked-for honor. I believed not
That thou wouldst deign to cast affection's eyes
On either of my daughters.

PRINCE. Deign! say rather
Aspire! for either merits the ambition
Of earth's supremest lords.

ERNALDO. Thy words have made me
Of fathers the most happy. But to whom
Shall I announce the honor of thy choice?

PRINCE. The Lady Isabelle.

REGINALD. Even so!

ERNALDO. For her,
I must confess that I had other views,
Which seem not to her liking.

PRINCE. And the cause
I can reveal; her heart to mine was plighted;
Nay, blame her not, for this was but concealed
Till fitting time should come for the avowal.

ERNALDO. I joy 't is come. The day that joins your hands
Shall be the proudest day of all my life.

REGINALD. Is it possible, my lord! Hast thou forgotten
The outrage he has done thee? Is it thus
He should be recompensed?

ERNALDO. He was in error,
And has atoned it. I am satisfied;

But it appears thy leave must first be asked, sir.
PRINCE. She comes, my beautiful!

*Enter* ISABELLE *and* JULIA.

ERNALDO. Now, Reginald,
Think not that I am ignorant of thy motives,
Or thy unuttered wish. Thou lovest my daughter,
And thou art free to woo her; should her love
Requite thee, she is thine, nor prince nor king
Shall wrest her from thee.
REGINALD. Thou but bidst me woo her
In mockery; but I am resolved to hear
My sentence from her lips. I cannot boast
Of lordly birth or proud inheritance;
All I can offer thee is but a heart
Where love enthrones thee, and before thee bends
As to its earthly god.
ISABELLE. [*To the* PRINCE.] Do me the favor
To bid that saucy boy speak to his equals.
REGINALD. Furies!
ERNALDO. But thou wilt give this princely suitor
A gentler answer?
ISABELLE. There is no disgrace
In his alliance.
ERNALDO. [*To the* PRINCE.] She is thine.
REGINALD. She thine!

No, never! Dare but touch her hand—by Heaven
I 'll make thee tremble!

ERNALDO. More respect.

REGINALD. Away!
Stir not thy tongue to chide me; I 'll not bear it,
Old man, I will not.

ERNALDO. Leave the house.

REGINALD. I shall, sir.
Now am I free, and my delivered spirit
Dances in buoyant joy. There 's none on earth
Whose word or frown I care for.

ERNALDO. Let us leave him. [*Exit.*

REGINALD. I leave you, and forever. Here no face
I care to seek again but thine, [*To the* PRINCE.] nor thine
In kindness. Darest thou meet me?

PRINCE. I shall give thee
A present answer.

ISABELLE. Prince, respect thyself
More than to notice him, a beggarly outcast.

REGINALD. A beggarly outcast! Well, I shall remember
Those words, and so shalt thou; they shall become,
To thee, as awful as the damning word
That welcomes from this world the guilty spirit.

JULIA. [*Soothing him.*] Dear Reginald!

REGINALD. There shall be done a deed
For which there is no name; and when 't is done,
And thou inquirest whose this deed——I laugh

Even now to think how I shall triumph then,
To yell in answer——Mine! the beggarly outcast's!
JULIA. Be calm, dear Reginald.
REGINALD. Calm as the whirlwind!
Fly me!—I would not harm thee—but I feel
As I could tear to pieces all around us,
Myself and thee.
JULIA. Dear Reginald!
ISABELLE. He 's welcome
To spend his rage in words.
REGINALD. Words!—deeds!—such deeds!
Think me not powerless, though bereft of all—
No country mine, nor kindred, not a friend—
Love, honor, happiness, nor even a home
Is mine—but thou, Revenge! thou shalt be mine,
Though from the lowest depths of hell I call thee!
THE STRANGER. [*Reappearing.*] It comes!
JULIA. God shield us!
REGINALD. If thou bringest revenge,
Thou art as welcome as a messenger
To heaven.
STRANGER. Nay, *there* I cannot be thy herald;
But I can lead to vengeance. [*Exit.*
REGINALD. On! I follow!
JULIA. [*Clinging to* REGINALD.] My friend, my brother, stay! in pity hear me,
And go not with that bad and terrible man!
REGINALD. Off! troublesome girl.

ISABELLE. Sister, for shame!

JULIA. Thou shalt not,—
Thou shalt not go.

STRANGER. [*Without.*] Reginald!

REGINALD. Hark! I come!
Revenge is mine!

[JULIA *falls, as he breaks from her and rushes away.*

CURTAIN DROPS.

---

## ACT III.

SCENE I.—*Night. A Storm.* THE STRANGER *is discovered on the brink of a precipice overhanging a river.*

STRANGER. Howl on, ye maddened elements! your groans
That shake creation, sooner shall be swallowed
In eve's soft whispering zephyrs, than shall drown
The eternal voice within me. Every sound
Has been opposed to this, and all in vain!
The shock of armies on the embattled field,
The blast of glory's trump, the thunder-burst
Of thronged applause, the adulation breathed
From kneeling myriads, the melody
Angelical, the lips of beauty bathing,

Or trembling from the strings that dance beneath
Her alabaster fingers—all by thee,
Merciless conscience!—all are overpowered,
And thou art heard alone!—Why then, all hail!
Tormentor welcome! I disdain to shrink
From horrors that with fiends I laugh upon
When others writhe beneath them;—shall they laugh
To mock my own?—they dare not—they shall tremble!

*Enter* REGINALD.

STRANGER. [*Descending the rocks.*] At last he comes, the unconscious instrument
Of *my* revenge.

REGINALD. Who names revenge?—Oh welcome!—
Speak! speak! instruct me in some deed unearthly
To make me for the infernal goddess Vengeance
A blood-anointed priest, and my example
The utmost that to the incarnate furies
Could seem desirable of imitation.

STRANGER. We shall attend to this within a moment.

RENINALD. This moment.

STRANGER. I must first—

REGINALD. Why dost thou vex me
With trifling? Can I heed thee while a tempest,
To which were this around us calm as Eden,
Maddens my heart to bursting!—Hence—lead on—

I care not whither, so it lead to vengeance!

STRANGER. Be patient; give me time, that I may shape
An object for thy vengeance, so sublime
In horror, hell's angelic host shall clap
Their gloomy wings applausive.

REGINALD. Yes, I 'd wait
For ages, so the sum of my revenge
Increased with every moment. [*Exeunt.*

SCENE 2.—*A room in* ERNALDO'S *palace.*

*Enter* ERNALDO.

ERNALDO. Happy Ernaldo! thy illustrious house
Now links to royalty!—Oh very happy!
Hell yawns before me, and a blood-robed phantom
Is ever near to plunge me in the abyss.
A diadem upon this aching brow
Could be no charm against him, or my conscience.
Who shall preserve me from them?—Oh ye heavens!
'T is said that ye are merciful and mighty,
Mighty to save, and merciful to pardon—
If ye are merciful, why am I thus?
Have I not knelt for mercy, prayed for mercy,
And wept for mercy? From this iron heart
What tears have not been wrung, and all for mercy—
What mercy have I found?

*Enter* JULIA.

ERNALDO. Who's there? My daughter,
What brings thee hither from the blithesome circle
Where all is gay festivity?

JULIA. My duty.

ERNALDO. Let that be made appear.

JULIA. I saw thee turn
From all the merriment with clouded brow;
I know the cause—

ERNALDO. Now God forbid!

JULIA. My father,
I followed to implore thou wouldst remove
Thy sorrow and its cause.

ERNALDO. [*Bitterly.*] Who can remove it?

JULIA. Though Reginald was worthy blame, thy heart
Repents the moment's rigor that has driven
The boy of thy adoption from thy house,
I know 't is this afflicts thee.

ERNALDO. I am sorry
For what hath past; but he may thank himself;
Let him abide the consequence.

JULIA. Ah no!
Thy heart speaks other language; I implore thee
Obey its better counsel; send for him,
Forgive him and receive him to thy favor—
Say, wilt thou not, dear father?

ERNALDO. Why, thou pleadest
With more than filial love.

JULIA. He was my brother,

My only brother; was he not to thee
A son? hast thou another to supply
His place in thy affections?

ERNALDO. Or in thine?
Ha! girl! thou lovest him?

JULIA. As a sister should.

ERNALDO. Thy tone speaks further than thy words. Nay, prithee
My girl, forbear that look distressed; I read
Thy heart, and blame it not. My other views
For Reginald have failed; thy innocent love
Shall well redeem their failure. Do I err?
Art thou unwilling to be his?

JULIA. Thy pleasure
Is all I seek, dear father.

ERNALDO. When the same
As thine, ha! wench? I wish the boy were here
To see that baby face, where smiles and tears
Make mirth of one another. Let us seek
The festive band; the merriest of them all
Shall find a match in one of us—ha! daughter! [*Exeunt.*

SCENE 3.—*The hermitage in the ruined castle.*

*Enter* THERESA *and* MANUEL.

MANUEL. Where is that evil man? What has he said
To make thy countenance so sorrowful?
Mother, believe it not.

THERESA. Alas! too well
I know its truth.

MANUEL. Oh for a warrior's sword!
Oh for a giant's arm! that I might thank him
For adding to thy sorrows.

THERESA. Hush, my child;
I would not any, thou the least of all,
Should harm a hair of his head.

*Enter* REGINALD *following* THE STRANGER.

REGINALD. Ha! what are these?
Ernaldo's wife and child! what do they here?

STRANGER. Thou art deceived; nor this Ernaldo's wife,
Nor this his child.

REGINALD. Whose then?

STRANGER. Boy, ask thy mother.

MANUEL. Yes, mother, tell me now what oft in vain
I 've asked of thee.

THERESA. Few nobler are in birth
And none in spirit, than thy father was,
His generous virtues and his high achievements
A nation voiced in triumph, as defying
The world to match her favorite son.

MANUEL. Oh mother!
How proud I should be of him,

THERESA. But there came
An earthquake on his soul, whose terrible

Revulsion, overthrew and buried all
His better feelings.

MANUEL. Whose unholy work
Was that? heaven's curse upon them!

THERESA. His high estate
And fortune measureless, tempted a villain
To his destruction.

MANUEL. Damn him!

THERESA. Hush!

STRANGER. Proceed.

THERESA. One eve, returning from a pleasant ride,
My husband and myself, and our young child
Were set upon by villains; our attendants
Dispersed or slain, I fled with womanish weakness,
But by the feelings of a wife and mother
Recalled, I hastened back—the child was gone—
My husband—

MANUEL. Oh not dead!

THERESA. My shrieks attracted
The inmates of a neighboring cottage; thither
They bore my husband's body; by our care
He was at last restored.

MANUEL. Thank God.

THERESA. His life
Continued in suspense. Spare me the rest.

STRANGER. It better suits my tongue. When he recovered,
His wife—imprudent wretch!—she told him whose

The murderous arm that struck him; from that moment
His soul became a hell, whose ruling demon
Was vengeance. But in vain for many a year
He sought the murderer, who in guilty terror
Had fled the country, even without securing
The fruits he sinned for.

MANUEL. And my father then
Went home and claimed his own?

STRANGER. No: he was careful
That his existence should be kept a secret
From all, lest it should reach his destined victim
And warn him to escape. Meantime to forward
His views, he joined himself to vile banditti.

MANUEL. Oh pitiful!

STRANGER. He soon became their greatest
In prowess and in guilt; he roved with them
From clime to clime, and like a conqueror's
His path was tracked with blood.

MANUEL. Alas, my mother!
Didst thou attend such scenes!

THERESA. I little knew
That such were passing. When thy father left me
He told not whither he would go or why.
Years passed; he came again, and I imagined
Guiltless as ever. He continued with me
Till thou wast born, but soon abruptly left us
Nor since returned.

STRANGER. For he was called away

By tidings that at last his destined victim
Had publicly appeared, and as his heir
Assumed his name, his title and his fortunes.
But still pursuit was vain, until the wars
In which an honorable part was borne
By the usurper, ending, he retired
To his usurped domains.

MANUEL, And there he fell
Beneath my father's arm?

STRANGER. No: the avenger
Restrained himself, to study direr pangs
Than death can give. But oft to slake his soul
Burning with enmity to all mankind,
He plunged in guiltless blood.

MANUEL. Oh tell me, mother,
Tell me that he deceives me, that a wretch
So wicked and dishonored, could not be
The father of thy Manuel.

STRANGER. By whose fault
Became thy father wicked and dishonored?
By hers!—Had she concealed the assassin's name,
The spirit of revenge had slumbered still,
Being without an object, and thy father
Had still been innocent and honorable.

THERESA. Forgive me! [*Sobbing.*

STRANGER. Damn thee! aye when God forgives me
Will I forgive thee!—Boy, I must avenge
Thy father's ruined soul. [*Stabs her.*

MANUEL. Oh, kill me too!
But thou, [*To* REGINALD.] I charge thee, as thou art a man,
Visit our blood upon him!

THERESA. Hush, my Manuel,
Speak not a word against him. Heaven forgive me
As I forgive him.

MANUEL. Oh my angel mother!
I cannot let thee leave me.

THERESA. Nearer—nearer—
I 'll waft thy kiss to heaven, and there I trust
It shall be rendered back. Where art thou?

MANUEL. Here,
My dearest mother.

THERESA. From my misted eyes
Thou fadest like a vision—yet I feel
Thy kisses on my cheek—one more—farewell—
God bless thee, my sweet boy!

MANUEL. Look there!

[*The* STRANGER *makes a signal, at which some attendants enter.*

STRANGER. Remove them!

MANUEL. Punish that wicked man.

STRANGER. Begone!

[*Exeunt attendants with the body, dragging* MANUEL *with them.*

And now, sir,
What thinkest thou of this lesson?

REGINALD. I must think

Thou art a master-fiend.

STRANGER. That woman's sin
Was worthy death.

REGINALD. What do they merit then,
By whom I have been frenzied?

STRANGER. Worse than death.
Wouldst slay the Prince?

REGINALD. Oh yes!

STRANGER. How pitiful!
Death but inflicts one pang, and by that one
Averts a myriad.

REGINALD. But I must have blood
To quench this raging fire.

STRANGER. And thou shalt have it,
But not the Prince's.

REGINALD. Whose?

STRANGER. His destined bride's.

REGINALD. Ah!

STRANGER. Dost thou shudder, fool?

REGINALD. [*Faltering.*] Poor Isabelle!

STRANGER. Poor Reginald! those are the very words
She whispers now to thy more happy rival;
For even at this late hour a brilliant throng
Are celebrating in Ernaldo's halls
The approaching nuptials, and the amorous pair
Belike bestow a thought of pity on thee
Amid their revelry.

REGINALD. Curse on their pity!

Come, we shall revel too; but it shall be
In blood.

STRANGER. In Isabelle's?

REGINALD. I care not whose. [*Exeunt.*

SCENE 4.—*A hall in* ERNALDO'S *palace, splendidly decorated and illuminated.* ERNALDO, ISABELLE, JULIA, *the* PRINCE, *and a throng of lords and ladies are discovered.*

ERNALDO. What dulls the merriment? Come girl, 't is thine, [*To* JULIA.
To waken it with one of thy sweet songs,
That well might waken death.

OMNES. A song! a song!

JULIA. Father—

ERNALDO. I 'll be obey'd.

OMNES. A song! a song!

JULIA *sings.*

What is the sweetest feeling
That ever on the soul
Of youth or maiden stealing,
Bids waves of rapture roll?
What the sublimest pleasure
Of those embowered above?
Or earth's divinest treasure?
'T is love! immortal love!

[*Chorus of youths and maidens.*

What are the ties most holy
  That link this happy pair?
And what the bliss that solely
  To know on earth they care?
And what the charm to either
  Shall seem all charms above,
Which time can sweep from neither?
  'T is love! immortal love! [*Chorus.*

ERNALDO. Well, girl—

JULIA. Excuse me, for I am opprest
With faintness, and have need to be relieved
By the fresh air.

A CAVALIER. Permit me?

[*Offering his arm, which she accepts, and retires with him.*

ERNALDO. Lords and dames,
Let this not break your pastime.—Music there!
Strike up a dance, and let our marble walls
Shake to the bound of merry feet.—What now?

[*To an attendant, who enters and approaches* ERNALDO.

ATTENDANT. Entering the chamber where I had committed
The lady and the child entrusted to me,
I found them gone.

ERNALDO. Why, let them go! I care not.

[*Attendant retires*

Fear, danger, sorrow, from this happy hour

Shall never trouble me. Strike up, I say!

[*A dance. The* STRANGER *and* REGINALD *enter and stand apart unnoticed.*

STRANGER. A joyous sight.

REGINALD. How maddening is the mirth
Of all around us, when we ourselves are wretched!

STRANGER. We 'll turn their mirth to mourning.

REGINALD. Look—see there—
She smiles like heaven!

STRANGER. She smiles upon thy rival.

REGINALD. Curse on her and her smiles! angelic devil!
See—see—his arm entwines her!—well! may this
Of mine drop from me, but he shall repent it!
They laugh!—Oh I could tear them!

STRANGER. Haply thou
And thy aspiring love provoked that burst
Of merriment.

REGINALD. My time shall come!

STRANGER. Observe
They steal away together.

REGINALD. And together
They die!

STRANGER. Be cautious, and in silence follow.

[*They retire unperceived, in the same direction as the* PRINCE *and* ISABELLE. *Scene changes to a garden, by moonlight. Enter the* STRANGER *and* REGINALD.

STRANGER. We have lost their track.

REGINALD. But like a raging lion
I 'll range in every place, till I have found them
Within my fangs.

STRANGER. Patience; await them here,
For they must pass this way. Dost thou remember
How I employed this dagger?

REGINALD. I shall prove
Upon the accursed Prince, I can employ it
As well.

STRANGER. That as thou wilt; but Isabelle
*Must* die.

REGINALD. They both shall die.

STRANGER. I hear their steps.
Remember. [*Retiring.*

REGINALD. 'T is resolved.

[*A* CAVALIER *and* LADY *pass by.*

LADY. How beautiful
Appears the face of Heaven!

CAVALIER. Like thine!

LADY. I never
Saw fairer sight. [*They pass on.*

REGINALD. Ye skies! how dare ye smile
In mockery of horror! Ye beauteous stars!
Young eyes of Heaven! ye do profane yourselves
If ye do look upon me!—Arise! arise!
Ye shades of Hell arise! from earth and Heaven
Cover a deed whose darkness pales your own!

[*The* LADY *and* CAVALIER *again pass by.*

LADY. Shall we return?

REGINALD. They must not pass in safety
This time; my baffled vengeance shall not be
Their jest.—Ho there!—the beggarly outcast strikes!

[*Stabs the* LADY, *who falls with a shriek; the* CAVALIER *supports her;* REGINALD *is about to stab him, when* MANUEL *rushes forward and catches his arm.*

MANUEL. Forbear! forbear!—Who sins against another
Sins most against himself.

*Enter* ERNALDO, *the* PRINCE, ISABELLE, CAVALIERS, LADIES, *and attendants, with torches.*

REGINALD. Too true thou speakest.
Oh Julia! have I slain thee!—thee of all
The only one that loved me!—Would to God
That I had loved thee sooner!

JULIA. Reginald!
Dear Reginald! such tender words from thee
Are cheaply bought with life.

ERNALDO. Where shall I turn
For comfort?

STRAGER. [*Advancing.*] Here!

ERNALDO. The might of agony
Sustains me in thy presence. Hast thou come
To drag me down to hell? behold me ready!
Such are my torments here, I cannot dread
An added pang hereafter.

STRANGER. Thanks, good brother!
Thou knowest not how much thy words delight me!
But I can tell thee something for thy comfort;
Thy weapon did not perfectly accomplish
Thy brotherly intent. Nay, I have lived
For vengeance yet; regard the scene before thee
And say, have I not lived to a good purpose?

REGINALD. Speak not of death, sweet girl!—there yet is hope—
'T is not a fatal wound; thou wilt recover—
Thou wilt—and I shall love thee—love thee dearly—
And all shall yet be well!

STRANGER. Thus I forbid it!

[*Stabbing* REGINALD, *who falls at* JULIA'S *side.*

ERNALDO. Oh miserable father!

STRANGER. Yes, I knew,
From the first moment that my eyes beheld him,
He was thy lawless son; and that impelled me
To study his perdition, as one means
Of cursing thee.

ERNALDO. [*Scarce able to articulate.*] 'T is not my son—
'T is thine!

[*The* STRANGER *stands gazing at* ERNALDO *for a moment; then rushes to him and drags him off the scene. All stand transfixed with horror, till startled by a wild cry without.*

CURTAIN DROPS.

LOVE'S YOUNG DREAM.

# LOVE'S YOUNG DREAM.

---

## THE FLOWER OF LOVE.

THAT we for riper years should stay,
  Though coldly thou declarest,
I tell thee, in the bloom of May
  The flower of love is fairest.
All who have loved must know the truth
  That love with time is flying;
It blooms but in the bloom of youth,
  Its power with beauty dying.
To beauty, by her magic strung,
  Love consecrates his lyre,
And none, except the fair and young,
  Its accents can inspire.
That we for riper years should stay,
  Though coldly thou declarest,
I tell thee in the bloom of May
  The flower of love is fairest!

## MY BLUE-EYED MAID.

WRITTEN AT THE AGE OF FOURTEEN.

Forget me not, my blue-eyed maid,
  When fate our parting shall decree!
My love may never be repaid,
  But still, oh, still remember me!
Thy image, in my heart enshrined
  In death's embrace alone shall fade;
When I am in his arms reclined,
  Forget me not, my blue-eyed maid!

If on the monumental stone
  The name of one thou chance to see,
Whose heart was thine, and thine alone,
  Oh then, my love, remember me,
As one that were supremely blest
  His life before thee to have laid,
Could that insure his last request:
  Forget me not, my blue-eyed maid

## MY FONDEST AND FAIREST.

My fondest and fairest!
  Oh why dost thou stay?
How can I be happy
  While thou art away?
I yearn to be with thee
  Wherever thou art—
My sweetest and dearest!
  Return to my heart!

My fondest and fairest!
  While sadly I cast
My glance round the scenes
  Where I looked on thee last,
Methinks I behold thee—
  To clasp thee I start—
My sweetest and dearest
  Return to my heart!

My fondest and fairest!
  No longer delay!
I 'm weary—I 'm wretched
  While thou art away!
Come! bring me the rapture
  None else can impart!
My sweetest and dearest!
  Return to my heart!

## THE CHARMS OF WOMAN.

THE glittering stars we admire,
  And the sun on his throne in the skies,
And we worship the lovelier fire
  That sparkles in woman's sweet eyes;
The bloom of the flourishing roses
  Delight to the eyes can impart;
And the bloom that dear woman discloses
  Has far more delight for the heart.

How sweetly the zephyrs are throwing
  The fragrance they snatch from the flowers!
How sweeter the breath that is flowing
  From the pure lips of woman to ours!
Whatever around thee thou meetest,
  The spell of delight that can lend,
The brightest, the fairest, the sweetest,
  In woman far lovelier blend.

Her eyes have a heavenly splendor,
  But if virtue have kindled its star
In her soul, its resplendence will lend her
  A light that is lovelier far!
Her breath has a sweetness when blending
  With ours in the pure kiss of love!
Far sweeter that breath when ascending
  In prayer to her Maker above.

When in one all the charms are united
  On the soul and the senses that steal,
When we gaze on her softness delighted,
  Or when to her brightness we kneel;
However those beauties may ravish,
  And fetter the soul and the eyes,
Not on them all our thoughts should we lavish,
  But spare one, at least, for the skies.

If the light of her eyes we admire,
  Oh, what is the glory of HIM,
From whom Heaven's eyes had the fire,
  To which even beauty's were dim!
Who the blaze to Apollo has given,
  Which the stars to behold cannot bear!
What splendor on earth or in Heaven
  Can with its Creator's compare!

If all the creation discloses
  Such beauty our homage to claim,
How awful a beauty reposes
  On the brow of the God whence it came!
When woman upon you has laid her
  Control, while you love and adore,
Oh, think of the BEING who made her,
  And love Him and worship Him more!

## THE GRAVE OF MARY.

Far, far from this grave be the footstep unholy,
 Its sanctity that would presume to invade!
By all who approach it, with reverence lowly,
 May homage to virtue and beauty be paid;

To virtue and beauty that almost had made her
 On earth, what they now have quite made her in heaven:
For the seraphic charms, in this world that arrayed her,
 To wither as soon as they bloomed were not given;—

Ah no! they were only transplanted again,
 To bloom in the glorious world whence they came;
Where nothing of earth or corruption shall stain
 Their splendors on high that eternally flame.

My Mary! my love! art thou hovering near
 To look upon him o'er thy dust who is kneeling,
While wrung from my bosom, full many a tear
 To water the grave of my Mary is stealing?

While o'er thee in passionate agony bending,
 I fondly would think, from the regions above,
Thy spirit I see in its beauty descending,
 To calm my wild anguish for Mary my love.

## MY OWN, MY CHOSEN BRIDE.

And thou art torn, my fairest!
From him who loves thee best,
And I must lose the heaven
That long my heart has blest!
But though we part, my fairest!
No parting can divide
Our wedded hearts, my fairest!
My own, my chosen bride!

Forget me not, my fairest!
Thou shalt not be forgot;
Remember all our fondness—
Sweet love! forget me not!
Where'er thou art, my fairest!
My soul is at thy side;
My heart with thine, my fairest!
My own, my chosen bride!

For years and years, my fairest!
A life of toil and care
Must win a worthy fortune,
For thee at last to share;
But then—oh then, my fairest!
I 'll come with joy and pride,
To claim my first, my fairest!
My own, my chosen bride!

## LOVE WITHOUT HOPE.

The meanest wretch that sullies earth
  May on thy beauty gaze,
And all unconscious of its worth
  May bask him in its blaze;
And those who care not for thy sight
  Their hours may by thee spend,
Where 't would emparadise me quite
  One moment to attend.

And those who to its charms are dead
  Thy angel voice may hear,
Which never shall its music shed
  For him who holds it dear!
And worthless fools the smile command
  That me with heaven would bless,
And heartless wretches clasp the hand
  That I would die to press!

But I who love thee—I to whom
  Thou art a saint below,
Ne'er to approach thee may presume
  Nor scarce a glance bestow;
I gaze when thou art gliding past,
  Unconscious of my eyes,
As gaze the lost at glimpses cast
  From opening Paradise!

Why should I seek thy heart to gain?
  Thy hand must be denied!
Why should they link affection's chain
  Whom fortune's gulfs divide?
Still shall I watch thee glide before,
  But bound my wishes there—
Such bliss is even this, that more
  Seems more than life could bear

## LOVE WILL FIND OUT THE WAY.

Though father and mother
  Forbid me thy sight,
Though sister and brother
  Against us unite,
Though all that surround us
  To part us essay,
From all will I win thee—
  Love will find out the way.

Though oceans may sunder,
  Or mountains may close,
Or tempests may thunder
  The path to oppose;
Though earthquakes between us
  The abyss may display,
Through all will I win thee—
  Love will find out the way.

Through forest and desert,
  Through flood and through flame,
Through pain and through peril,
  Through sorrow and shame,
Through darkness and danger,
  By night or by day,
Through death and destruction—
  Love will find out the way.

Yes, I will regain thee,
  My chosen, my best!
My bird! thou shalt nestle
  Again in my breast;
This heart for thy refuge,
  This arm for thy stay,
I will guard thee forever—
  Love will find out the way.

## MY LOVE LOVES ME.

Oh there is a song
  That the young heart sings!
That forth in a fountain
  Of music springs,
As fresh as the dance
  Of the streams set free—
"I love my love,
  And my love loves me!"

Sweetest and dearest,
  Fondest and best,
While with thy presence
  No longer blest,
My heart murmurs o'er
  As it strays to thee,—
"I love my love,
  And my love loves me!"

And thou, my beloved,
  When I leave thy sight,
It soothes me to think
  That thou wilt delight
To murmur the song
  I taught to thee,
"I love my love,
  And my love loves me!"

We heed not the pleasures
  To others known,
A better and dearer
  Is ours alone,
To whisper our hearts
  In their secret glee,—
"I love my love,
  And my love loves me!"

And oh! when again
  I welcome thy face,
When again I clasp thee
  In fond embrace,
To me wilt thou whisper,
  And I to thee,—
"I love my love,
  And my love loves me!"

## BROKEN TIES.

Go—I from my soul disclaim thee,
Mine I never more shall name thee;
By the love that thou hast slighted,
By the joy that thou hast blighted,
By the fairy visions vanished,
Ingrate! go, forever banished!

By the promise vainly spoken,
By the heart thou wouldst have broken,
Did not strength of soul sustain me,
That I mourn not but disdain thee,
Go, forever from me driven!
Go—forgotten—not forgiven!

When thou findest all around thee
Faithless, worthless, as I found thee,
Thou shalt learn the worth to measure
Of the heart thou wouldst not treasure;
But in vain thy soul's repentance—
Irrevocable the sentence—
Go, forever from me driven!
Go—forgotten—not forgiven!

## THE BEST AND THE WORST OF IT.

When to the crowded halls of mirth
  I turn, from lonely thoughts to fly,
And find the change but little worth,
Amid the throng alone on earth,
  For very sorrow I could die.

But when that heavenly face I see
  Whose loving looks to mine reply,
The world appears my own to be,
For she is all the world to me,
  And I for very joy could die.

When youthful dreams, forever fled,
  From memory claim the hopeless sigh;
When long lost friends like spectres tread,
  The cold, the faithless and the dead!"
  I feel so wretched I could die.

But when those eyes, in which I trace
  The beauty of the starlight sky,
Look up so fondly in my face,
All sweetness and confiding grace,
  I feel so happy I could die.

## THE LOCK OF HAIR.

She loved me well, whose precious head
This cherished ringlet bore;
Yet there will come a time I dread,
When she will love no more:
A thousand chances will occur
Her kindness to estrange;
This little lock is all of her
That time will never change!
And when the lip that once I prest
No smile to me will give,
This ringlet in my lonely breast
Shall bid some comfort live;
And when some happier heart shall bless
The love I must resign,
How will I prize this little tress,
*Unaltered* still and *mine!*
I have but little joy on earth
Or hope of joy above,
Save one that every joy is worth—
The Paradise of love:
Why must I know it will not last,
That fate will only spare,
Of all the love and rapture past,
One little lock of hair!

## I KNOW THAT THOU ART FAR AWAY.

I KNOW that thou art far away,
  Yet in my own despite,
My still expectant glances stray
  Inquiring for thy sight;
Though all too sure that thy sweet face
  Shall bless no glance of mine;
At every time, in every place,
  My eyes are seeking thine.

I hope—how vain the hope I know—
  That yet some blissful chance
May bring thee here, again to throw
  Thy sweetness on my glance;
But my best love, where'er thou art,
  Whate'er be my despair,
My eyes shall seek thee, and my heart
  Shall love thee everywhere.

## LOVE'S AMBITION.

FROM THE GERMAN OF CONRAD KREZ.

Oh that I were a king
  In golden pomp arrayed!
And thou, most beautiful,
  Wert but an humble maid;

Then would I say to thee,
  "Oh best beloved of mine,
Behold my crown and throne,
  For throne and crown are thine!

"In truth thou art not sprung
  From those of royal race,
But Nature's royalty
  Adorns thy form and face.

"I climbed the lofty heights—
  I found them drear and bare;
I sought the deepest vale—
  The sweetest flower was there!"

Now, from thy rosy mouth,
  I hear the gentle sound—
"Oh let that flower remain
  Still in its native ground!

"Its beauty and perfume
  Live in this mossy place;

Why break it off to die
  Within a golden vase?

"I ask not for my brow
  A coronet of pearls—
Give me a budding rose
  To place among my curls!"

I fling my sceptre far,
  Deep, in the deepest sea—
For what are crown and throne
  Without thy love for me?

'T is not a crown of gold
  Can match thy brighter hair—
'T is not a diamond wreath
  Can with thine eyes compare!

Had I as many crowns
  As shine the stars above—
Oh! I would give them all,
  Sweet maiden, for thy love!

And yet I must repeat—
  And thou wilt not upbraid—
Oh that I were a king,
  And thou an humble maid!

## WEDDED LOVE.

I MAY not call to grandeur's hall
  The lady of my heart;
I have not power or wealthy dower
  My true love to impart;
I bid her from a sphere to come
  That far is mine above;
Yet shall not this impair the bliss
  That hails our wedded love!

She will not grieve a home to leave
  Magnificent in pride,
In lowly cot to share my lot,
  Obscurely there to hide;
Though desolate of friend or mate,
  Save me and GOD above,
Yet shall not this impair the bliss
  That hails our wedded love.

She has been nurst among the first
  And proudest of the land,
Where from her head all danger fled,
  At fortune's magic wand:
But ill my bower in stormy hour
  Can shield my gentle dove;
Yet shall not this impair the bliss
  That hails our wedded love.

I every day a tender lay
  Shall waken to her name,
And every night to throne of might
  Shall kneel to bless the same;
For years and years, through smiles and tears,
  I 'll prize her all above;
And well shall this insure the bliss
  That hails our wedded love.

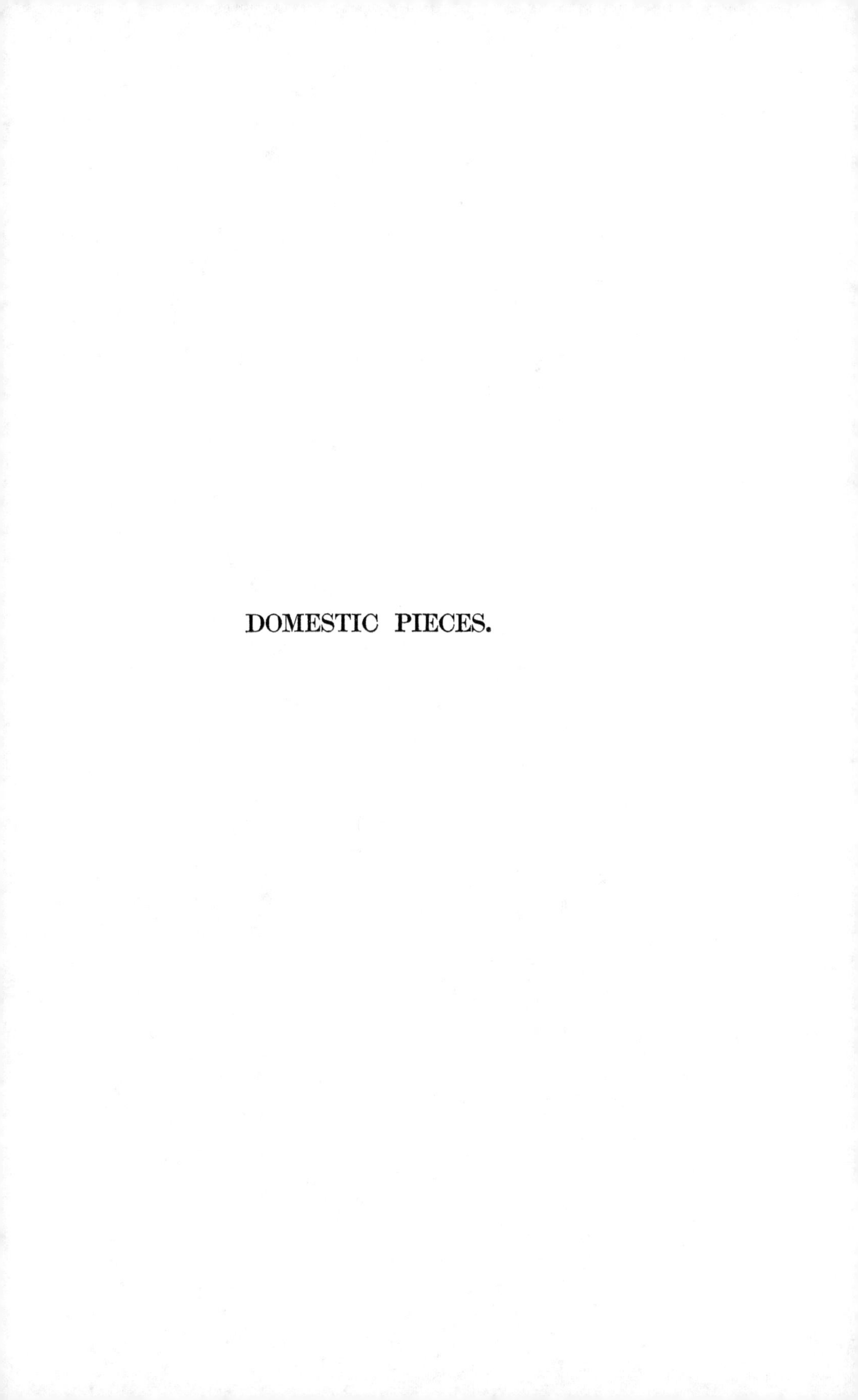

# DOMESTIC PIECES.

## DOMESTIC PIECES.

### A NEW-YEAR'S GREETING TO MY DAUGHTER.

So it is gone!—another year!
  A drop of time lost in the sea
  Of dark and deep eternity,
In which we all must disappear!
Well, since so transient our career,
The blessings that attend the way
More precious grow with every day:
  So is it with my EVELINE,
  And ever was since she was mine;
Since first she nestled on my breast,
And on its beatings rocked to rest;
And when her little arms at length
To twine around me gathered strength,
And her young eyes replied to mine
With love's intelligence divine;
When first her lips began to frame

Sweet murmurings of a father's name;
Or with more eloquence of love
  Those rosy lips to mine were prest—
Oh, closer still I clasped my dove,
  And could have died so very blest!

Years passed—the infant passed from sight—
  A glorious child stood in her place,
With golden curls and eyes of light,
  And fairy form and seraph face;
Her feet went dancing as they trod,
  In fullness of her heart's delight;
Her voice sent carols up to God—
I heard it not, but God knows best—
  I felt so happy, sure HE smiled
  In love on father as on child:
I know it, for we have been blest!
  And though at times we feel His rod,
He blest us, and we *shall* be blest!

My child, my friend, my playmate dear!
And dearer still with every year,
Since more and more I seem to find
An answering sympathy of mind,
My pleasures, hopes, and views that shares,
In part, my studies and my cares!
Oh, while we live, can each depend
At least on one unfailing friend!

For friendship, like a dream expires,
And love itself burns out its fires;
But who, my child, shall rend apart
The links that bind us heart to heart?
I 'll hold thee fast, whate'er my lot,
My child! my friend that faileth not!
And thou—betide thee good or ill—
Cling to me close and closer still,
And lay thy head upon my breast,
Thy refuge, and thy place of rest!

Roll on, ye years! if, as ye roll,
Ye bring more treasures to her soul!
I know not, and I care not much,
  How she may look to other eyes—
I praise her not for form or face;
  More happy far to recognize
The beauty which alone can touch
  The soul—the mind's immortal grace;
The heart, unknown to sin's control;
  The spirit robed in light divine,
Still soaring to its native place;—
  These be thy glories, EVELINE!
The wings that yet shall lift thee far
  Above the bondage of our clay,
And make thee as the Morning Star,
  That shineth unto perfect day!

## TO MY WIFE.

The winds of March are loose again,
  And shrinking, from the piercing air,
I shudder at the thought of pain
  That I have borne, and yet may bear;
But while the scenes return to view,
  Which seemed to be my last on earth,
Returns the heavenly picture too
  Of all thy love and all thy worth!

Thy matchless love, that bore thee up
  Through trials few have heart to brave;
That shrank not from the bitter cup
  Of anguish, which my anguish gave;
That, while thy noble heart was wrung
  With pity, tenderness, and grief,
Still o'er my couch of suffering hung,
  To give me comfort and relief.

A common love might weep and sigh,
  To spare its grief, my presence shun
And in its weakness let me die,
  Lamented much, but aided none;
Thy nobler nature rose above
  All trials, so they gave me aid,
And on the altar of thy love
  Thy heart a sacrifice was laid.

Thy sighs were hushed, thy tears supprest,
  Lest I thy sorrow should divine;
Thy eyes refused their needful rest,
  To watch the fitful sleep of mine:
No sharer in a task so dear
  And sacred would thy love allow;
By day and night, still hovering near,
  My "MINISTERING ANGEL" thou!

Thou wast my dearest hope on earth
  Since first I met thy welcome sight;
But never had I known thy worth
  Till in affliction's darkest night:
Oh, then thy peerless goodness shone,
  A star amid the gloom profound,
Dispersed the clouds above me thrown,
  And scattered heavenly radiance round.

The God of mercy heard thy prayer,
  When hope itself receded fast,
And gave to thy unwearied care
  The life that seemed already past;
That life I ever would employ
  To bless thee, and thy love repay,—
To give thee comfort, peace, and joy,—
  To be thy friend, thy shield, thy stay.

I will not at the past repine,
  Though the remembrance wakes a sigh—

To know the worth of love like thine
  'T were well to suffer or to die!
But ah! at once its worth to know
  And to enjoy its fullness, *live!*
No greater favor heaven can show,
  And earth has nothing more to give.

---

## SHE CALLS ME FATHER.

She calls me "father!"—though my ear
That thrilling name shall never hear,
Yet to my heart affection brings
The sound in sweet imaginings;
I feel its gushing music roll
The stream of rapture on my soul;
And when she starts to welcome me,
And when she totters to my knee,
And when she climbs it to embrace
My bosom for a hiding-place,
And when she nestling there reclines,
And with her arms my neck entwines,
And when her lips of roses seek
To press their sweetness on my cheek,
Or when upon my careful breast
I lull her to her cherub rest,
The heart to which I hold my dove
Swells with unutterable love!

## MY LITTLE DAUGHTER'S WELCOME.

THE world looks pleasantly and bright
Upon my new-born child;
The fields and skies are bathed in light,
The air is fresh and mild;
And it would seem all heaven and earth
Were gracious to my darling's birth!

May this her future lot foreshow!
Still may her skies be bright;
And every scene she treads below
Be pleasant to her sight.
So may she live on earth beloved
And cherished, and by heaven approved!

May all that smiles upon her now,
Smile on her to the end;
And when upon her placid brow
The shades of death descend,
To everlasting life reborn,
May she salute a brighter morn!

## A FATHER'S DIRGE.

My hopes are blighted, and I feel
An anguish I may not reveal;
  And fain I would retire apart
Where common eyes may not intrude,
Who care not for the sanctitude
  Of sorrow in a father's heart.
But I have duties to perform
  To others, who have claims as strong,
And still must struggle with the storm
Of life amid the careless throng;
And veil the secret of my breast
With smile for smile, and jest for jest,
While fain I would sink down to rest
  Beside my darling's clay!
Yes—for my wife and children's sake,
I 'll bid my energies awake,
And nerve the heart that swells to break,
  To be their shield and stay.

But, oh! the sorrow, when I come
From weary work to lonely home,
To miss that face, whose pleasant sight

Gave to that home a heavenly light!
At hour of rest, how sad to miss
The comfort of her parting kiss!
And every morning when I wake
This lonely heart is nigh to break,
For ever when I rose from sleep,
  Beside me smiled her cherub face,
And close and closer she would creep
  To nestle in my heart's embrace!
But now at every wonted spot
I seek her, and I find her not;
Save that at times before my eyes
Distempered fancy bids her rise
As last I saw her, night and day
Gasping her little life away!
And then my anguish and despair
Become too terrible to bear!

Yet, my beloved! though I must mourn,
  And nothing can my grief beguile,
I should rejoice that thou wast born
  To bless me though but for a while.
The love that lightened up thy eyes,
  And smiled on thy angelic face,
Was such a glimpse of Paradise,
  As though but for a little space,
A sacred influence has left
Of which we cannot be bereft,

And tell us what the heavens must be
That for a moment lent us thee,
And fires our zeal to persevere
To meet thee in that better sphere,
Where yet we trust redeemed to stand
And lead our darling by the hand,
Thou best of all our hearts held dear!

If thou canst see us from above,
At last thou knowest all the love,
  Nor words nor tears could tell;
Thou readest in thy father's heart,
Of which thou wast the dearest part,
  A love unspeakable!
And thou dost love me, my sweet child,
And thy affections from the skies
Come down to bless me, till I rise
To meet them pure and undefiled;
Oh, let me then be reconciled,
And conquer passion's bitterness,
  For why should we deplore
That earth has now one sufferer less,
  And heaven one angel more!

The sun rose glorious on thy birth,
  As if he welcomed thee to day,
And shone as glorious, when to earth
  We gave thy cold unconscious clay.

I saw him on his noonday throne,
  In summer's proudest hour,
And thought of all he looked upon,
  Thou wast the fairest flower!
Where art thou now?
                    Nay, it is weak,
'T is wrong, that gloomy grave to seek!—
Let Faith and Hope unveil the skies
A moment to affection's eyes!
Look up, my soul! and there behold
A heavenly form with locks of gold,
That shade a brow divinely bright,
And float upon her wings of light;
All Paradise is in her face,
And in her smile celestial grace;
She looks upon us from above
With pity and undying love,
And gently beckons to her home—
I come, my Anna!—soon I come!
And till we meet, will strive and pray
To keep upon the only way,
Nor more repine that thou dost rest
Upon a Heavenly Father's breast!

## THE WATCHES OF THE NIGHT.

In the watches of the night,
  When the world is hushed to sleep,
  Comes my anguish strong and deep,
Like a torrent at its height,
Rushing with resistless might,
  Every barrier down to sweep;
Parts the darkness like a veil,
  And reveals my dying dove,
With her patient face and pale,
  And her sweet blue eyes of love,
Sadly looking into mine,
Till they every look resign.
Now returns the scene of death—
Slowly gasps away her breath;
Now the lips that were my bliss
Move as for a parting kiss;
Now she gives a feeble start,
As to nestle to my heart!
  How its breaking fibres thrill!
All is over!—from my sight
Fades the vision of the night,
  And the night is darker still!

Day returns—thou swelling breast,
Hush! and hide thy sacred guest!
  Forth into the world I go—
Hollow laugh and ribald jest
  Round me bandy to and fro;
And I look and list the while
With a forced and feeble smile,
  Bitter mockery of woe!
Common talk of common things,
Like the buzz of insect wings,
Brushes o'er my weary mind,
And I answer in some kind,
  What I hardly care or know.

Nay, my soul, this is not well!
  Rouse thee from thy stern despair,
Crush the thoughts that would rebel,
  Nobly bear what thou *must* bear!
Leave it to the common crew
  In their sorrow to be weak;—
  In the might of anguish seek
Might to bear and might to do;
Gather up thy inmost strength—
  To some earnest task apply;
So shalt thou escape at length
  Thoughts that else would bid me die!

Thou from whom all blessings came!
Thou who dost at will reclaim!
Thou who the Great Father art,
And in every parent's breast
Strongest feelings hast imprest,
Sweetest, purest, holiest,
Yet canst rend a parent's heart,
Snapping all its links apart!
Thou who didst the boon bestow,
  Once my comfort, hope, and pride,
Yet removed it at a blow—
  May that blow be sanctified!
Though my heart is sorely tried—
  Though my hopes are in the dust,
In Thy wisdom I confide,
  In Thy boundless mercy trust!

## MY BOY.

My boy! my boy! what hopes and fears
Are prophets of thy future years!
How many smiles—how many tears
  Shall glisten o'er this face!
This eye, so innocently bright,
May kindle with a wilder light,
  In pleasure's maddening chase:
This brow, where quiet fancies lie,
May proudly lift itself on high,
  In fierce ambition's race;
This form, so beautiful, so blithe,
May waste in sickness, or may writhe
  In agony's embrace;
This cheek may lose its healthful blush,
For sorrow's languor, passion's flush,
  Or thought's corrosive trace;—
But of all evils that may come,
My prayer the most would shield thee from
  The guilty or the base.
Thy heritage is but my name;
Then prize its purity of fame,
  And shield it from disgrace;

And if that name have some renown,
May it be thine a brighter crown
  Upon it yet to place!
For should a prouder wreath be thine
  Than ever was or shall be mine,
  The more will be my joy—
The vanity of fame I 've found;
Still could I wish its laurels crowned,
  My boy! my only boy!

And yet, should genius never roll
Its inspiration on thy soul,
  Nor gift thee with the might
To image such creations forth
As crown the "Minstrel of the North,"*
  Imperishably bright;
Or with a Shakspeare's muse of fire
Up to the highest heaven aspire,
  The sun of every sight—
If science shall not in thy mind
Unfold a beacon to mankind,
  Amid the mental night;
Or if thy arm shall never wield
A hero's sword, on conquest's field,
  To guard thy country's right—
If all the glorious hopes be vain
That often float athwart my brain

* Walter Scott.

In visions of delight—
Still thou as fully canst complete
The hope—of all most dear and sweet
That may my mind employ—
All other wreaths I can resign,
So virtue's trophies may be thine,
My boy! my only boy!

---

## A VALENTINE TO MY WIFE.

Twelve years ago! how swift their flight,
Since first thy fate was linked with mine;
How much they brought of dark or bright
To crown thy love, or prove its might,
My faithful Valentine!

Twelve years ago, my chosen bride!
How proud was I to call thee mine!
But more my love, and more my pride,
Since years on years thy worth have tried,
My precious Valentine!

It may be sorrow and despair
  At times have wrung this heart of mine;
But to thy love I could repair,
And find my peace and solace there,
    My sweetest Valentine!

And every joy that I may know,
  When kinder fortune seems to shine,
Wins from thy smile a brighter glow—
To see thee happy makes me so,
    My dearest Valentine!

Sweet mother of the cherub boy,
  Round whom our fondest hopes entwine!
May he his coming years employ
To be thy comfort, pride, and joy,
    And bless my Valentine!

## MY BABE.

My babe! my own, my precious babe!
  When I behold thy charms,
And look upon the mother sweet
  That folds thee in her arms,
It seems to me as I possessed
  The richest treasures here—
For she is best of all the best,
  Thou, dearest of the dear!

My babe! I have but little store
  Of what most mortals prize;
And thousands pranked in pomp and pride
  My humbler lot despise—
Yet thinking of my wife and child,
  A prouder head I rear,
Blest with the best of all the best
  And dearest of the dear!

My babe! thou hast no heritage
  Except thy father's name,
Which in misfortune's worst despite
  Has won its way to fame;

And fame is only precious, that
  It serves the lot to cheer
Of these, the best of all the best,
  And dearest of the dear.

My babe! if all my little store
  Should in a moment end,
Should slander blast thy father's fame—
  Forsake him every friend,—
Thy mother spared and thou, his head
  Above the storm would rear,
Blest with the best of all the best,
  And dearest of the dear!

My babe! in all thy path of life
  Thy mother's steps pursue,
And let the pattern of her worth
  Be ever in thy view;
So shall thy father's heart be glad
  And proud of thy career,
And thou be best of all the best,
  And dearest of the dear!

## MY DARLING LITTLE MARY.

When childhood shall have flown away,
  And youth its bloom shall lend thee,
May all the bliss of childhood's day
  And innocence attend thee;
Nor may a heart so pure and blest
  For guilt or sorrow vary,
That now are strangers to thy breast,
  My darling little Mary.

When beauty's glow is on thee thrown,
  May it be thy endeavor
Not outward charms to win alone,
  But those that perish never.
Since all the charms that meet the eye
  Are not more bright than airy,
Be thine the charms that never die,
  My darling little Mary.

On earth may Mary long repay
  The fondness of a mother;
And from this world when called away
  By death to seek another,
May angels her pure spirit bear
  To bliss that cannot vary,
And may a mother welcome there
  Her darling little Mary!

## THE MOTHER'S PRIDE.

YES, she is beautiful indeed!
  The soft blue eyes, the golden hair,
The brow where pleasant thoughts we read,
  The radiant smile, the winning air,
The cherub form of perfect grace,
  Whose fairy steps in music glide—
And oh! that sweet, that heavenly face!
  Well may she be her mother's pride!

Yet may she nobler pride awake
  Than all external charms impart;
'T is not alone for beauty's sake
  We hold her in our inmost heart—
Her sunny soul, her spotless mind,
  Where comes no thought to shun or hide,
Her artless love, her feelings kind,
  Have made her more her mother's pride.

Then come to me, my blue-eyed child,
  And bending o'er my shoulder, fling
Thy golden tresses, rolling wild,
  In many a soft and sunny ring!
Look up in fondness to my face,
  And thine upon my bosom hide,—
Close—closer, to my heart's embrace,
  My sweetest joy!—my fondest pride!

## THE FONT.

No boon that fortune can impart
  May with a gracious child compare;
It winds into the parent's heart,
  And twines with every fibre there.

When to my arms my children spring,
  Or on my breast their heads recline,
Or to my lips of love they cling,
  No joy on earth can equal mine.

Yet e'en on these so fair and dear,
  Whose looks are more of heaven than earth,
Some shadow will at times appear,
  Some stain that speaks of mortal birth.

But there is an immortal stream
  That cleanseth every stain away;
And where those living waters gleam,
  All darkness brightens into day.

And thither we our children bring,
  To Him who said, "Forbid them not!"
That He within that sacred spring,
  May cleanse their souls from every spot.

Saviour of all! who in the charms
  Of childhood once this world hast trod!
We bring our treasures to Thy arms,
  And dedicate them to our God!

## THE NAMESAKE.

I HAVE a little daughter
 Is only two years old,
Her eyes are blue as heaven,
 Her locks like sunny gold!
Her soft and fair complexion
 Might every heart enthrall,
But 't is her sweet affection
 I value more than all;
For dearly does she love me,
 And in my heart I hold
My charming little daughter,
 That 's only two years old.

In other years to bless me
 A youthful vision came,
As lovely and bewitching
 As one who bears her name;
And while upon my daughter
 I look with fondest gaze,
Again returns the vision
 That blest my early days!
While nestling on my bosom
 Looks up her face serene,
It seems that GOD restores me
 My long-lost JOSEPHINE!

Oh! that it were no vision!
  That I might near thee stand,
Again thy fairy fingers
  To clasp in friendship's hand!
Oh, wert thou but a moment
  Returned to my embrace!
Oh, that I but a moment
  Could see thee face to face!
Look in thy eyes' blue heaven,
  The golden curls remove,
And press on thy pure forehead
  The seal of perfect love!

## ON THE DEATH OF A YOUNG SISTER.

But yesterday a child of pain,
That saddened pity's eye—
To-day, a seraph called to reign
Above the stars on high!
Well might the suffering move our tears,
Which she endured below;
But now that heaven her soul inspheres,
Those tears should cease to flow.

Why should we her release deplore
From fate's relentless arm?
Why grieve that she shall grieve no more?
As if we wished her harm!
Away with the repining tear,
The ingrate sigh forbear,
Which if she up in heaven could hear,
Would grieve her even there!

Yet Nature's voice, more mighty far
Than all the rest can say,
Still calls us from the radiant star,
Down to the mouldering clay;

And not in words the magic lies,
  To calm the anguish wild,
Of one whose lonely heart replies,—
  "It was my child! my child!"

And GOD, who knows a mother's heart—
  Permits a mother's tears,
When from the cherub doomed to part,
  The holiest tie endears;
And JESUS an example gave,
  All feeling hearts accept;
Weep on—for at Affection's grave,
  The PRINCE OF GLORY wept!

That we have lost her we may weep;
  Yet knowing she is blest—
That all her cares are hushed to sleep
  Upon her SAVIOUR'S breast—
That thought with its consoling power,
  Amid our tears shall gleam,
Like rainbow in a summer shower,
  Or moonlight on a stream.

Her calm submission to the rod,
  Which made all else repine,
Revealed her as a child of GOD,
  While yet on earth, divine!
With sweetest thoughts of heavenly birth,
  Her sainted mind was fed,

Which flung a glory, not of earth,
  Around her dying bed!

May we from her example learn
  Submission to our lot,
And to the Rock of Ages turn,
  Whose promise faileth not!
So shall our sorrows pave the way
  To the eternal home,
Where our beloved has gone to-day,
  And seems to whisper, "Come!"

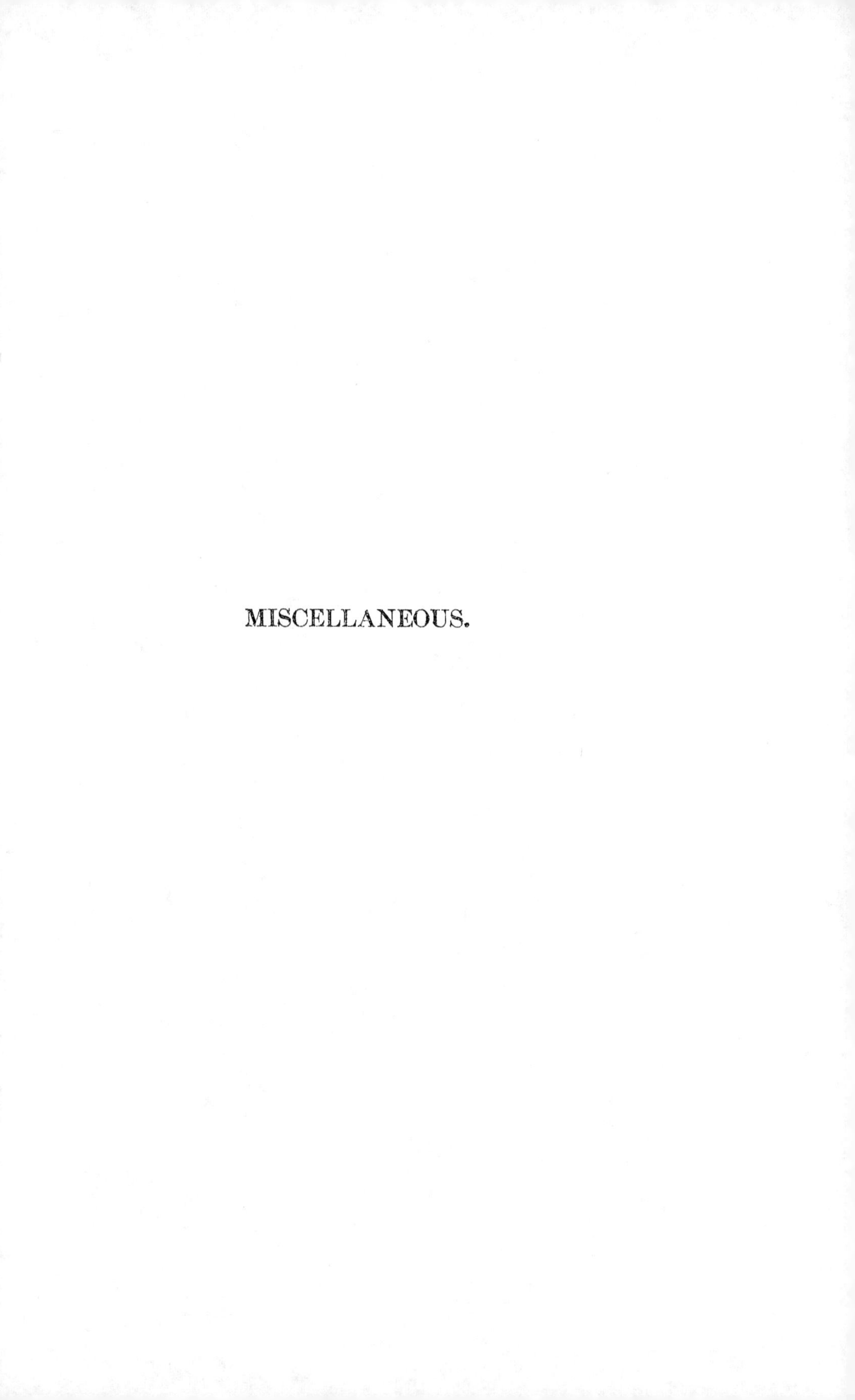

# MISCELLANEOUS.

# MISCELLANEOUS.

---

## TO CHARLES DICKENS.

FRIEND of my heart!—friend of the human race!
Though I may never gaze upon thy face,
Nor clasp the hand that has such wonders penned;
  Yet when entranced by thy prevailing spell,
    I watch the ebbing life of gentle *Paul*,
    Or looking up, as at an angel's call,
  Pursue the heavenward flight of "*Little Nell*,"
Heart leaps to heart, and I embrace my FRIEND!

It hath been given to thy hand to trace
All that is good and glorious in our race;
As with an "angel's ken" thou hast divined
The riches in the human heart enshrined;
Crowns, sceptres, laurel wreaths, or robes of state,
Thy genius needs not to reveal the great.

Greatness is only greatness *in itself*,—
  It rests not in externals, nor its worth

Derives from gorgeous pomp, or glittering pelf,
  Or chance of arms, or accident of birth;
It lays its deep foundations in the soul,
  And piles a tower of virtues to the skies,
Around whose pinnacle majestic, roll
  The clouds of glory, starred with angel eyes!

Such is the lofty lesson thou hast taught,
But still diviner blessings hast thou wrought;
Like light from heaven, thy genius has unveiled
  Affection's deepest mystery of grief,
  And to despairing sorrow brought relief,
Where reason and philosophy had failed,
By opening the fountains of the heart:
And therefore distant strangers give thee part
In their affections, as a household guest,
Who shares the sacred secret of their breast.

There is a sorrow that can never die;
  There is a loss we never can forget,
Yet can it purify and sanctify,
  And mingle heavenly solace with regret;
And therefore do we love thee and thy page,
Which moves our tears, but moves them to assuage;
And therefore do I hail thee as my friend,
  And yield the tribute of a grateful heart;
Though humble is the offering I send,
  Affection may some little worth impart.

## PASSING THE CHURCH.

Oft as I pass St. Thomas' Church,
  A kindly glance I throw
Where sleeps a friend I daily met,
  "Some twenty years ago."

And thinking of those happy times,
  As slowly past I wend,
I scarce forbear to touch my hat,
  And say, "Good morning, friend!"

Nor is it with uncheerful mind
  That I his memory greet—
More years have past since we have met
  Than shall before we meet.

And sweetly placid seems his rest,
  Though near his silent bed
The tide of life rolls thundering by,
  As it would wake the dead.

Who knows but yet some consciousness
  May linger under ground?
Who knows but yet, with genial smile,
  He looks on all around?

The busy throngs, beset with cares
It once was his to know—
The dashing belles, who rival those
He loved so long ago.

And hark the heavy tramp of steeds—
Of men the measured tread—
The clang of trumps—the roll of drums—
Wake, soldier!—lift thy head!

Bright weapons glitter in the sun;
Proud banners flout the sky;
Up, soldier! mount thy prancing steed,
And wave thy sword on high!

In vain—Earth could not tempt him back
With all that pleased him best—
For better worth than all she gave,
His calm and quiet rest!

And, therefore, in the city's midst,
Serenely doth he lie,
Regardless of the storm of life
That rushes madly by.

For me—far from the city's din,
Be mine some rustic tomb,
Where trees shall wave above the sod,
And flowers around it bloom.

Life's bustling scenes have been to me
  But scenes of pain and care—
I would not have them round my bed,
  When I am sleeping there!

Yet friendly steps will seek my grave,
  Wherever that may be;
And loving lips shall bless my name,
  As now—unheard by me!

No want of fervent tears or prayers,
  Could those recall me here—
But what can love or friendship say
  To death's regardless ear?

Up, Poet!—Glory bids thee rise!—
  Death shall not keep thee down!
Up, Poet!—strike the harp divine,
  And wear the immortal crown!

Rise!—Earth restores all thou hast lost—
  Fame—fortune—beauty's smile!
Unheeded proffers!—though the last
  Might tempt me for a while!

But speak not *thou*, my chosen one!
  Of all beloved the best!
For *Love* is stronger than the grave!
  And thine would break my rest!

## THE BEST OF COUNSEL

### TO THE BEST OF GIRLS.

Now heed my words, my precious girl!—
Affection is the richest pearl,
Nor lightly should be thrown away
On those who cannot love repay;
Beware to whom thou shalt impart
That priceless jewel of the heart!
Care not alone for form or face,
Or winning words or witching grace;
But choose thou one whose honored name
Thou canst be proud to share and claim;
Let it be one of cultured mind,
Of generous thoughts and feelings kind,
Who never sought, nor e'er would seek
To wrong the helpless or the weak,
But ever would employ his best
To shield the friendless and opprest;
Who proudly treads temptation down,
Nor sinks at fortune's darkest frown;
Whose equal soul and mind sedate
Can stand unmoved each change of fate;
Whose faith is firm, whose honor bright,
Whose love is an immortal light!
Such were the love, and such alone,
That can be worthy of thy own!

## TO GERTRUDE.

I LOVE thee!—need I say it now?
  Not for the eye of heavenly blue,
Not for the fair transparent brow
  Which azure streams meander through,—
The roseate cheek, the raven curls
  That round the breathing marble dance,—
For those adorn a thousand girls
  Who scarce attract my passing glance!
Though thine is beauty's fairest flower,
  And all the magic she imparts,
It is not *that* which gives thee power
  To wind into my heart of hearts!

I love thee for thy gentle mind
  Where thought of evil hath no place,
Thy grateful heart, thy feelings kind,
  Thy modesty's bewitching grace!
Thy pure affection's welcome rush,
  That laves my fevered soul in bland
Refreshment, like the fountain's gush
  To Arabs 'mid the burning sand.

I love thee by my perfect trust
  In that affection's perfect truth;
My hopes have crumbled oft in dust,
  And friends have failed me from my youth;
Though time may common hearts estrange,
  And common friends their ties may break,
There is a heart can never change,
  A friend that never will forsake!

I love thee—not with passion's fire,
  But the devotion pure and high,
A guardian seraph might inspire,
  Who came with comfort from the sky!
There is a blight upon my heart,
  A hopeless sorrow on my mind—
But GERTRUDE! dearest! where thou art
  I seem the peace of heaven to find!

Oh may the peace of heaven be thine,
  Sweet GERTRUDE! be what may my lot!
When life and thee I must resign,
  Remember—yet lament me not!
E'en then be happy in the thought
  That thou hast loved me to the end;
For thou hast been the boon I sought,—
  A chosen and a faithful friend!

## WOMAN'S MINISTRY.

'T is true that love's romantic dreams
Are bright as heaven's opening gleams,
And give to life a charm divine,
That wisdom sorrows to resign;
Yet much they err who seek in this
The only or the highest bliss,
Or deem that woman's noblest part
Is but to give and win a heart.
This angel (such in all but wings)
Was born for higher, holier things,
And best her ministry fulfills
In smoothing life's pervading ills.
'T is hers to soothe the troubled mind,
'T is hers the broken heart to bind,
To turn the erring soul to prayer,
And snatch the sinner from despair;
To hover round affliction's bed,
With angel look and fairy tread;
Receive affection's dying breath,
And seal the cherished eyes in death!
And all the while forbear to show
The sorrows God alone can know!
The spirit thus sublimes the clay,
All selfish taint refines away,
Till too divine to be concealed,
The perfect angel stands revealed!

## WALTER SCOTT AND WASHINGTON IRVING.

God bless thee, Walter Scott!
  For thou hast blest mankind,
And flung upon their lot
  The brightness of thy mind,
And filled the soul with pleasures
  None other can impart,
And stored the mind with treasures,
  And purified the heart.

Shame on them who abuse
  Their gifts of peerless price,
And prostitute the muse
  To passion or to vice!
Who pour into the mind
  The bitterness and gall
Which makes us hate mankind,
  Ourselves, and heaven, and all!
We leave their withering page,
  For *thine*, with healing rife,
The fevered soul assuage,
  And drink the stream of life!
Thy shrine is virtue's altar,
  Thy fame without a blot;
God bless thee, dear Sir Walter!
  God bless thee, Walter Scott!

One only son of light
  Attends thy cloudless path,
In purity as bright
  As thy own spirit hath;
To charm away distress,
  To comfort, to delight,
To teach, to aid, to bless,
  He shares thy wizard might!
His muse from virtue's shrine
  Hath never turned astray,
Nor ever breathed a line
  That love could wish away;
The temple of the free
  Is radiant with his fame,
His country's glory he—
  And IRVING is his name.

God's blessings on ye both!
  Twin heirs of glory's prize!
How often when I loath
  All that around me lies,—
When in the crowded world
  I feel myself alone,
From all communion hurled
  That by the rest is known,
Debarred, by fate's control,
  From every human sound,
And burying my soul

In solitude profound—
Oh, then, ye glorious pair!
I seek the world ye give,
And find a kindred there
With whom I love to live,
Your precious magic nerving
My soul to bear its lot—
God bless thee, gentle IRVING!
God bless thee, WALTER SCOTT!

## THE BELL SONG.

PARTLY FROM THE LIED VON DER GLOCKE.

Above the scenes of earthly labor,
  In heaven's clear vault, the blue, the bright,
She swings on high, the thunder's neighbor,
  And borders on the world of light,
Where roll the stars in circling mazes,
  Her voice responding to their song,
While they repeat their Maker's praises,
  And lead the crowned year along.

Her iron tongue, in earnest measure,
  Speaks of the solemn and sublime,
And hourly warns us of the treasure
  We hourly waste, unvalued time!
To destiny a voice imparting,
  She swings, its changes to proclaim,
And hither, thither, swiftly starting,
  Keeps time to life's inconstant game.

Ring out! ring out a joyous greeting,
  In welcome to the lovely child,
Whose little heart begins its beating
  In slumber's arms, the undefiled!

His future lot of gloom or splendor
Is curtained from his vision tender;
A mother's love, her best adorning,
Keeps watch upon his golden morning.

Years speed like darts—for scenes of strife
  Proud youth from girlhood fiercely sunders,
Plunges into the storms of life,
  And wanders through the world of wonders;
A stranger to his father's home
  Returning, lo! in youthful splendor,
All-glorious as an angel come
  From heaven, with bashful look and tender,
And blushing like the orient skies,
  The maiden stands before his eyes!

His heart is seized with nameless yearning;
  He turns aside; alone he strays;
His eyes with sudden tears are burning;
  Again he turns to seek her gaze,
And blushingly her pathway traces
  Until her greeting makes him blest;
He seeks the fairest flower, and places
  Its beauty on her fairer breast!

Young love! what longing hopes unfoldeth
  Thy golden time! what joys of price!
The eye an open heaven beholdeth,

And swells the heart in Paradise!
Young love! ah, couldst thou ever nourish
The golden dream! for ever flourish!

Let him, enthralled by passion strong,
Approve, before the lasting union,
If heart with heart is in communion;
The dream is short, repentance long!

Ring out! ring out! for triumph blesses
The youth who by the altar stands,
And lovely in the young bride's tresses
The nuptial wreath entwines its bands.
Alas! that life's enraptured fire
Should with the May of life decay,
The fairy dreams of young desire
With veil and girdle rent away!

Flits passion's hour;
Yet love remaineth,
A ripening flower
Which truth sustaineth.
Into hostile life
Man forth must enter;
In toil and strife
His thoughts must centre;
In planting and making,
Pursuing and taking,

Risking and daring,
Plotting and caring,
And running his race
In fortune's chase.

He prospers:—fortune rolls a boundless tide;
His stores increase; expands his dwelling wide;
And therein ruleth
The matron chaste,
The children's mother,
With wisdom graced;
In her circle moving,
Smiling or reproving,
The little girl directing,
The little boy correcting,
She plies her busy fingers
With work that never lingers;
Her husband's gains increases
With toil that never ceases,
And fills the closets with fragrant stores,
And spins at the wheel that rolls and snores,
And piles the wardrobe's well-polished row
With the shining wool, and the flax of snow,
And joins with the showy the useful ever,
And resteth—never!

The father with a glance of pride
Looks from his far-extended dwelling,

And counts his gains on every side,
  And views his stores with treasures swelling;
Then boasting lifts his haughty hand—
"Firm as the earth's foundations stand,
Against misfortune's rudest shock,
My house is founded on a rock!"
Vain boast! who can resist an hour
To destiny's almighty power!

Ring out! a fearful peal ring out,
To second terror's frantic shout!
  Hark! the crashing thunder
  Rends the skies asunder!
Lightnings quiver, flash, and shiver,
And roll through heaven a blazing river;
Earth reflects the burning flood,
Glow the skies as red as blood,
  But not with glow of day;
Yet the night is glaring bright
As the sun's meridian light:
      The clamor of dismay
        Higher swells and higher;
Loud and loud the bell is rung,
Flies the cry from tongue to tongue,
      "Fire! fire! fire!"

Lo! a pyramid of flame
Fierce as if from hell it came,

Clouds of smoke around it curled,
Soars as if to show the world
Creation's funeral pyre!
Lo! unconquerably strong
Rolls the burning flood along,
While the air around its path
Glows as with an oven's wrath—
Fire! fire! fire!

Sinks the roof and totters wall,
Pillars shake and columns fall;
Treasure won by toil of years
In a moment disappears;
All are running, rushing, flying,
Shouting, shrieking, trembling, crying;
Beneath the smoking ruins crushed
The beast is moaning,
The child is groaning,
Till both in suffocation hushed.

But steady stand an active band—
The buckets fly from hand to hand,
And from the toiling engine rushes
A cataract in showery gushes:
In vain—in vain—
The splashing rain
The mighty element devours
In scorn;—then gathering up its powers
As if from laboring earth

A Titan struggled into birth,
Towers giant-like on high;
And helpless, to its godlike strength
Man yields the hopeless strife at length,
And stands all idly by,
While the possessions, late his trust,
Melt like a shriveled scroll in dust.

One backward glance he calmly throws
Upon his fortune's grave,
Then turns away in stern repose,
His coming fate to brave.
Though destiny her power has proved,
She spares him still the best of blisses;
He counts the heads of his beloved,
And lo! not one dear head he misses!

Ring out! ring out!
Sad and slow
Tolls the bell
The dirge of woe,
In solemn train, a band of mourning friends
A wanderer to the home of all attends.
Alas! the wife! the fond, the cherished!
The faithful mother! she has perished!
From her husband's arms for ever
The Prince of Terrors bids her sever,
And bears her with his shadowy hand,

From amid the tender band,
Which she in blooming beauty bore
To him, whom she may bless no more;
And on her bosom nourishing,
Watched enraptured flourishing,
With the love, the pride, the pleasure,
Mother-hearts alone can measure.

Ah, tender ties of home! ye sever!
  For she who was the house's mother
In bed of darkness sleeps for ever,
  And now her place receives another!
Poor orphans! where her gentle guidance?
  Her tender care all else above?
Ah! where she ruled a stranger ruleth,
  Whose love is—*not* a mother's love! *

Ring out! ring out! a peal of dread!
  Sound trumpet! thunder drum!
Wake—rise—prepare for battle's bed!
  The foe! they come! they come!
All start in a bewildered dream,
And woman's shriek, and childhood's scream
  Half drown the bell's alarms;
While youth and manhood hasten out,

* Thus far I have done little more than paraphrase select passages from the German poem. What follows, I have added to complete the idea I had in view.

And rush, and run, and storm, and shout—
  "To arms! to arms! to arms!"

A thousand torches scatter light
On scenes of fury or affright;
While women, with disheveled hair
And wringing hands, dart here and there,
And weep and clamor, loud and wild,
All helpless as the wondering child;
Or others with seraphic eye
Look up, and trust in God on high,
Pale, breathless, silent, and sublime,
Like statue of the Grecian time!
And others bowed in weeping prayer,
Invoke a heavenly Father's care.

Good God! who would not die for these—
The cherub child that clasps our knees,
  The wife of angel charms,
The virgin, fresh in beauty's glow,
The home, our Paradise below—
  To arms! to arms! to arms!

A thousand mingled weapons clash
And quiver in the torch's flash;
Some grasp the sword, the musket some,
The axe, the spade, whate'er may come
  To the unfurnished hand:
Staff, club, or missile—all may serve—

No weapon but the arm can nerve
 To guard its native land.

Hark! the storm of battle!
 Guns and cannons thunder
 As earth would rend asunder;
Bullets whiz and rattle,
 Showering death around;
 Thousands press the ground,
And groan away their souls;
 Every sword is ruddy,
 Every hand is bloody,
And Carnage o'er the field her iron chariot rolls.

See the foe receding
 From the victor's might;
See the hero leading
 To pursue their flight;
See the warrior bleeding,
 Struggling still to fight—
On the field disabled lying,
See he grasps his weapon dying,
 Shouting, while from the battle storm,
The foes, confusedly flying,
 Trample upon his mangled form,
Lightnings flashing from the eyes
 Closed in death that soon shall be,
 "Victory!
 Victory!"

Away he springs
On conquest's wings,
And in the bright embrace of glory dies!

Ring out! ring out a solemn peal,
While to the King of kings we kneel,
Through whom our arms prevail!
Each soldier bends his laureled brow,
And bows the knee no foe could bow—
Hail! God of Armies! hail!

Around him kneel the wife, the mother,
The child, caressing each the other;
Their cheeks, but now so pale,
With triumph flushing, while their eyes
In rapture swimming seek the skies—
Hail! God of Glory! hail!

Ring out! a glorious peal ring out!
While like a rushing storm we rise,
And stand erect, and rend the skies
With one triumphant shout!
Hurrah!
Ring out! ring out in tone sublime—
How awful swells the glorious chime!
While blending with its tones, we raise
To God one choral song of praise,
To God, the Father of the free,
Who giveth us the victory!

## MY CHILDHOOD.

WRITTEN AT THE AGE OF FIFTEEN.

My childhood scenes! oh, where are they?
  I now am but in boyhood's years,
Yet on no scene my glance can stray
  To memory one trace endears
  Of childhood's smiles, or childhood's tears;
I look at every spot so strange,—
  So altered now,—and then I say,
While pained my heart remarks the change,
  "My childhood scenes! oh, where are they?"

My childhood friends! oh, where are they?
  The dearest in the grave recline,
And others, long estranged away,
  Forget they e'er were friends of mine;
  And yet I never can resign
The memory of even such
  As least repaid affection's sway;
But still this thought my soul must touch,
  "My childhood friends! oh, where are they?"

My childhood joys! oh, where are they?
  And where the innocence, which gave
To every joy its purest ray?
  Those joys have found an early grave;—
  That innocence!—oh could I save
The innocence of childhood's hour,
  Not thus should I be sorrow's prey,
Nor sigh beneath affliction's shower,
  "My childhood joys! oh, where are they?"

Where is my childhood now? and where
  Shall be my youth?—its every joy?
Its every scene?—But spare, oh spare
  Its friends, though time all else destroy!
  And if some feelings yet employ
My mind, which heaven may pure esteem,
  Oh! may I not the horror bear
To say, when launched on manhood's stream,
  "Where are such feelings now! oh, where?"

## TO CORDELIA.

Bright eyes, fair tresses, cherub faces,
And forms that paragon the Graces,
Are found in twenty thousand places.

But for a mind of gifted splendor,
A heart confiding, true, and tender,
The world has very few to render.

Those treasures are to thee imparted,
For thou on life's career hast started,
With gifted mind and open-hearted.

A name is thine that lives for ages,
And every sympathy engages,
On Shakspeare's consecrated pages.

Cordelia! true and faithful ever,
Whose love and duty wavered never!
Her sainted name shall live for ever!

And all that we in her admire,
Should duty call or love require,
Thy generous bosom will inspire.

But may no grief like hers attend thee,
But every joy that earth can lend thee,
And every good that heaven can send thee.

Come to my heart! and closer pressing,
Receive, if it be worth possessing,
A poet's love, a poet's blessing.

## ALONE.

NAY, ask not of the secret grief
  That burns my heart away,
For what admits of no relief
  'T is useless to betray;
One cause for gloom might well appear,
  Were all the rest unknown—
Where'er I am, whoe'er be near,
  I am alone!—alone!

At times I seek some festive place,
  Where gay companions throng,
While pleasure brightens every face
  With laugh, and jest, and song;
But lost to me the cheerful sound,
  Unheard the kindly tone,
And with a thousand friends around
  I am alone!—alone!

Yet there is one who had a charm
  My sadness to dispel,
When round me twined her gentle arm,
  With love no words could tell,—
A love that seemed to have no will
  Or wish except my own—
Oh, Clara! might I meet thee still,
  I should not feel alone!

Young, beautiful, and innocent,
  Her very sight could bless!
Her looks, than words more eloquent,
  Did all her thoughts express;
And then I did not feel the curse
  That on my lot is thrown;
For soul with soul did we converse,
  And I was not alone!

But Youth is still a thing of light
  And joy.—Why should I doom
A cherub God has made so bright,
  To share my lonely gloom?
Though all the comfort thou couldst lend,
  That may to me be known,
Go, Clara! seek some happier friend,
  And leave me all alone!

---

## THE DIFFERENCE.

Man strides along through thick and thin,
Through miry shame and thorny sin;
With careless hand the thorn or spot
He brushes off, and all 's forgot;
But woman, soft and delicate,
At every step must hesitate—
The fallen man again can soar,
But woman falls, to rise no more.

## THE PEARL-HANDLED KNIFE.

A LITTLE boy sits by his mother's tomb,
And waters the flowers that above her bloom,
With tears that flow from his orphaned heart,
Sobbing as if it would burst apart.

He looks around with a glance of fear,
To see that no ruthless eye is near,
Then draws from his bosom his cherished toy,
His mother's last gift to her own dear boy:
It was a knife with a silver blade,
And of mother-of-pearl was the handle made.

That little boy has a step-dame stern,
Whose evil feelings against him burn;
Though once on the orphan boy she smiled,
And kindly treated her husband's child;
But a change was on her feelings thrown
When she had a little babe of her own,
For she loved her babe with a love so great,
Her love for the orphan was turned to hate:
For it was thought she could not bear
That Edwin should be his father's heir;

"And all would be for my child," she said,
In her guilty heart, "were but Edwin dead!"

Oh! a mother's love is a holy thing!
But even from good may evil spring,
And they who would love with a sinless love,
Must set their affections on things above,
Nor ever, for perishing things of clay,
From God and his law be led astray.

Poor Edwin! he found it a cruel change,
For all was bitter and all was strange;
Now first in his life he felt and heard
The passionate blow and the angry word,
And knew not what it could mean the while,
For he had been ruled by look and smile.

His father had gone abroad for a time
To gather wealth in a distant clime,
And Edwin was left in his step-dame's power,
Who beat and abused him every hour.
But once in a day the orphan fed,
And then on a bone or a crust of bread;
His strength decayed, and a fever came,
But it made no change in the ruthless dame;
She spurned him up as he sunk on the floor,
From which he gladly would rise no more;
And she made him work like the veriest slave—
How he longed to rest in his mother's grave!

To that mother's grave he crawled one day,
When he thought the dreaded eye away,
And told her unconscious ear the wrong
Her poor little boy had endured so long;
Then drew from a secret slit in his vest
The only comfort he yet possest;
It was a knife with a silver blade,
And of mother-of-pearl was the handle made.

Alas! for the cruel step-dame was near,
And heard what he meant for his mother's ear;
On her evil mind temptation flashed:
At a blow the boy to the earth she dashed,—
She snatched the knife with a sudden start,
And buried the blade in the orphan's heart.

She opened the door of his mother's tomb,
And thrust him down in that place of gloom;
She hastened home and she laughed so wild—
"Come kiss me! all is your own, my child!"

A month elapsed, and the father came,
And kissed his babe and his smiling dame;
But when he asked for his pretty boy,
To deepest sorrow it changed his joy;
"The child," she said, "of a fever died,
And was buried at his mother's side."

A year and another passed away,
And the babe grew lovelier every day:

It was a bright and a merry child,
And the father of half his grief beguiled.
Another year and another past,
And the child in beauty flourished fast,
And the father's heart no more was sad,
And the mother's heart was proud and glad:
She forgot her sin, as too many do,
And fancied God had forgot it too.
A guilty deed may be long concealed,
But its time shall come to be revealed,
And long unpunished may flourish crime,
But vengeance cometh in God's good time.

It was a fair and a sunny day,
And Robert went in the fields to play;
But the shades of night began to fall
Before he returned to his father's hall—
"Oh, Robert! where have you been so long?
My child, to wander so late is wrong."
"Mamma, I am sorry I stayed so late,—
This morning I passed by the churchyard gate,
And found it open; I wandered there,
To gather the flowers so fresh and fair;
And weary at last with my play alone,
I laid me down on the nearest stone.
I had not been resting long, before
I noticed a tomb with a little door:
Oh, mother! I gazed in fear and doubt,

For opened the door and a boy stept out;
But when his beauty beamed on my sight,
My fear gave way to a strange delight.
His cheek was fair as the sunset skies
And like stars of heaven, his sparkling eyes:
Adown his shoulders his ringlets rolled,
And glistened and gleamed in sunny gold;
But the charm all other charms above,
Was the smile that melted the heart to love;
Yet was it a sad and a serious smile,
And the tears would start to your eyes the while.

He came where I lay;—he spoke—the sound
Breathed music in all the air around;
He lay at my side, and he took my hand,
And he talked of a brighter and better land,
Where nothing of evil can enter in,
Nor sickness nor death, nor sorrow nor sin;
Where God's holy children, a radiant band,
In his garden of glory walk hand in hand;
Where all is bliss, and all is love—
And he whispered—'Oh, come to my home above!'

And thus we talked till the close of day,
And then we arose to go away;
But he flung his arms around me mother,
And kissed my forehead, and called me—'Brother!'
And as he turned to descend the grave,
He gave me a keepsake—see what he gave!"

The mother looked—with a frantic start
She plunged it into her guilty heart—
It was a knife with a silver blade,
And of mother-of-pearl was the handle made.

## THE BATTLE OF THE SNAKES.

### AN EPISTLE TO CATHARINE.

DEAR KATE—more dear than I can tell!
No matter though—you know it well—
Dear Kate—in this delicious weather,
I wish, don't you? we were together;
That we might wander, hand in hand,
Amid those scenes of fairy land,
Which now to glad thy vision rise,
And fancy pictures to my eyes;
To climb the hills, the woods explore,
Or ramble by the sea-beat shore,
Where ringing waves delight thy ear
With music mine shall never hear:
Or rove where sweetest flowers embower
My pretty Kate, "a sweeter flower!"
While balmy zephyrs kiss thy brow
Of beauty—(might I kiss it now!)

'Mid scenes like these, one summer's day,
A lordly serpent wound his way;

From Rattler's line of length he came,
And gloried in a tail of fame;
His pointed tongue, his sparkling eyes,
His gorgeous robe of thousand dyes—
All these with rapture swelled his hide,
For snakes, like other fools, have pride.
While winding through a tangled brake,
He chanced to meet another snake,
Who wore a suit of sober black,
Which might become a doctor's back,
And coiled in many a ring, reclined,
While thoughts as coiled perplexed his mind.
"Good Parson Black! ah, is it you?"
Quoth flippant Rattle, "How d' ye do?"
"I 'm pretty well, I thank you, sir."
"How 's Mrs. Black?" "All 's well with her."
"How are the little dears?" "So so;
The youngest has been ailing though."
"How go the times?" "Oh, very bad!"
Sighed Black; "the times are truly sad,
Which plunges me in deep dejection,
And makes me ask in sage reflection,
Why all that is beneath the skies,
Is what it is—not otherwise!
Why Providence, by strange mistakes,
Instead of men, has made us snakes;
Why we are born—and wherefore die—
Why——" "Fool!" quoth Rattle, "care not why!

He who himself will wretched make
Deserves the hiss of every snake,
Enough for us that all on earth
Is full of beauty, life, and mirth;
While of its joys I have a share,
I care not who may cherish care—
Mine be the maxim wise and just:
'Live while you live, die when you must!'"
"Then die this moment!" Black exclaimed,
With foaming lip and eye inflamed.
At this the other shook his rattle,
To sound the stirring charge to battle.
So fiercely they together flew,
They bit each other right in two.
Quoth Black, "I beg a truce, my friend,
To ponder on my latter end!"
So each in different windings past,
To seek his tail, and fix it fast;
But in their hurry, by mistake,
Black got the tail of Rattlesnake,
And Rattle to himself did tack,
Unwittingly the tail of Black.
  Now Rattle fiercely shook the tail
He thought his own, without avail,
To wake the sound once wont to be
His "earthquake voice of victory!"
Now right, now left, he lashed the ground,
But burn the tail! it gave no sound!

He swings it left, he swings it right—
In vain, poor Rattle bursts with spite.
  Black, for his part, had run away!
But as he runs, to his dismay,
Loud from his tail a rattle peals,
As if the foe were at his heels.
More fast he runs, more loud it rings,
And louder, as he faster springs:
He runs for six successive suns,
And still it rattles as he runs:
He runs and runs till out of breath,
And then the rattle sleeps in death.
  You say this story can't be true—
Dear Kate, I quite agree with you!
But now that I must say farewell,
One little word of truth I 'll tell;
And well you know I speak sincerely,
In saying, "*Kate, I love you dearly!*"

Postscript. Some say they are not able
To see the moral of my fable!
Inform them, had the snakes been wise
'T is like they would have *used their eyes!*
And secondly, it hence appears,
Our eyes are better than our ears;
From which reflection I contrive
Some consolation to derive;
For though I oft have sighed, my dear

That it is not for me to hear
The thrilling music of thy voice,
That would my very heart rejoice:
Yet when my arm is round thee wreathing,
And on thy brow my lip is breathing,
When thy dear head my hand caresses,
Or wreathes among thy raven tresses,
Or clasps in mine thy fairy fingers,
While fond my look upon thee lingers,
Then, while emparadised, I trace
Affection breathing from thy face—
Oh, then I feel in deep delight,
There is a music for the sight!
Which I would not exchange for all
That ever on the ear may fall.

# CATCHING A FOX.

## A FABLE.

INSCRIBED TO MY LITTLE FRIEND CATHARINE.

THE rise of provisions, and hardness of times,
Had thinned a poor fox like a stringer of rhymes,
And thinner and thinner became the poor sinner,
With never a penny to get him a dinner;
(For me, when I come to that sorrowful state,
I know where to go—to my own little Kate.)
But the fox only went, with a sigh and a shiver,
To drink, like a temperance man, at the river;
When, hark! from the stream came a musical voice,
Disturbing his reverie sad—
Rejoice! rejoice!
Rejoice! rejoice!
Oh! is not an oyster a clever lad?"

The fox turned round with a cheerful gleam,
And dipped his tail in the cooling stream,
And twitched and twirled it with all his might,
But never a fish was the fool to bite;
This the oyster saw, while his merry voice
Repeated the chorus glad:

"Rejoice! rejoice!
Rejoice! rejoice!
Oh! is not an oyster a clever lad?"

Thought the oyster, "Now is the time for glory,
And to win a name in historic story!
This mighty fox shall my triumph grace,
And my fame shall shine on the oyster race."
This said, he snapped at the fox's tail,
While all the fishes stood mute and pale.
"Sir fox," says he, with exulting voice,
"I guess you are caught, egad!
Rejoice! rejoice!
Rejoice! rejoice!
Oh! is not an oyster a clever lad!"

Away from the river sped the fox,
Nor stopped till he came to a pile of rocks,
Then he swung his tail right fast and well,
And banged the oyster out of his shell,
And ate him up for a dinner choice,
And chuckled the chorus glad,
"Rejoice! rejoice!
Rejoice! rejoice!
Oh! is not an oyster a clever lad!"

## THE OLD CLOCK.

Two Yankee wags, one summer day,
Stopped at a tavern on their way,
Supped, frolicked, late retired to rest,
And woke to breakfast on the best.

The breakfast over, Tom and Will
Sent for the landlord and the bill;
Will looked it over: "Very right—
But hold! what wonder meets my sight!
Tom! the surprise is quite a shock!"
"What wonder? where?"—"The clock! the clock!"

Tom and the landlord in amaze
Stared at the clock with stupid gaze,
And for a moment neither spoke;
At last the landlord silence broke—

"You mean the clock that 's ticking there?
I see no wonder I declare;
Though may be, if the truth were told,
'T is rather ugly—somewhat old;
Yet time it keeps to half a minute;
But, if you please, what wonder's in it?"
"Tom; don't you recollect," said Will,
"The clock at Jersey, near the mill,

The very image of this present,
With which I won the wager pleasant?"
Will ended with a knowing wink—
Tom scratched his head and tried to think.
"Sir, begging pardon for inquiring,"
The landlord said, with grin admiring.
"What wager was it?"

"You remember
It happened, Tom, in last December,
In sport I bet a Jersey Blue
That it was more than he could do,
To make his finger go and come
In keeping with the pendulum,
Repeating, till one hour should close,
Still, '*Here she goes—and there she goes!*'
He lost the bet in half a minute."
"Well, if *I* would, the deuce is in it?"
Exclaimed the landlord; "try me yet,
And fifty dollars be the bet,"
"Agreed; but we will play some trick
To make you of the bargain sick!"

"I'm up to that!" "Don't make us wait,
Begin. The clock is striking eight."
He seats himself, and left and right
His finger wags with all its might,
And hoarse his voice and hoarser grows
With—"*here she goes—and there she goes!*"

"Hold!" said the Yankee, "plank the ready!"
The landlord wagged his finger steady,
While his left hand, as well as able,
Conveyed a purse upon the table.
"Tom, with the money let 's be off!"
This made the landlord only scoff!
He heard them running down the stair,
But was not tempted from his chair;
Thought he, "The fools! I 'll bite them yet!
So poor a trick sha'n't win the bet."
And loud and loud the chorus rose
Of, "*Here she goes—and there she goes!*"
While right and left hls finger swung,
In keeping to his clock and tongue.

His mother happened in, to see
Her daughter; "where is *Mrs. B——?*
When will she come, as you suppose?
Son!"
"*Here she goes—and there she goes!*"

"Here?—where?"—the lady in surprise
His finger followed with her eyes;
"Son, why that steady gaze and sad?
Those words—that motion—are you mad?
But here 's your wife—perhaps she knows
And"——
"*Here she goes—and there she goes!*"

His wife surveyed him with alarm,
And rushed to him and seized his arm;
He shook her off, and to and fro
His finger persevered to go,
While curled his very nose with ire,
That *she* against him should conspire,
And with more furious tone arose
The "*here she goes—and there she goes!*"

"Lawks!" screamed the wife, "I'm in a whirl!
Run down and bring the little girl;
She is his darling, and who knows
But"——
"*Here she goes—and there she goes!*"

"Lawks! he is mad! what made him thus?
Good Lord! what will become of us?
Run for a doctor—run—run—run—
For Doctor Brown, and Doctor Dun,
And Doctor Black, and Doctor White,
And Doctor Grey, with all your might."
The doctors came, and looked and wondered,
And shook their heads, and paused and pondered,
Till one proposed he should be bled,
"No—leeched you mean"—the other said—
"Clap on a blister," roared another,
"No—cup him"—"No—trepan him, brother!"
A sixth would recommend a purge,
The next would an emetic urge,

The eighth, just come from a dissection,
His verdict gave for an injection;
The last produced a box of pills,
A certain cure for earthly ills;
"I had a patient yesternight,"
Quoth he, "and wretched was her plight,
And as the only means to save her
Three dozen patent pills I gave her,
And by to-morrow I suppose
That"——
"*Here she goes—and there she goes!*"

"You all are fools," the lady said,
"The way is, just to shave his head.
Run, bid the barber come anon"—
"Thanks mother," thought her clever son,
"*You* help the knaves that would have bit me,
But all creation sha'n't outwit me!"
This to himself, while to and fro
His finger perseveres to go,
And from his lip no accent flows
But, "*here she goes—and there she goes!*"

The barber came—"Lord help him! what
A queerish customer I 've got!
But we must do our best to save him—
So hold him, gemmen, while I shave him!"

But here the doctors interpose—
"A woman never"——
"*There she goes!*"

"A woman is no judge of physic,
Not even when her baby *is* sick.
He must be bled"—"No—no—a blister"—
"A purge you mean"—"I say a clyster"—
"No—cup him—" "Leech him—" "Pills! pills! pills!"
And all the house the uproar fills.

What means that smile? what means that shiver?
The landlord's limbs with rapture quiver,
And triumph brightens up his face—
His finger yet shall win the race!
The clock is on the stroke of nine—
And up he starts——"'T is mine! 't is mine!"
"What do you mean?"
"I mean the fifty!
I never spent an hour so thrifty;
But you, who tried to make me lose,
Go burst with envy, if you choose!
But how is this? where are they?"
"Who?"
"The gentlemen—I mean the two
Came yesterday—are they below?"
"They galloped off an hour ago."
"Oh, purge me! blister! shave and bleed!
For, hang the knaves, I 'm mad indeed!"

## THE MAGIC RING.

I HAD a magic ring,
  A charm of wondrous power,
If placed on fitting hand,
  And in a fitting hour:
For, to a worthy hand,
  This talisman would bring
Good fortune and renown,
  And every precious thing;
And youth and beauty's grace
  Forever would preserve,
But only to the face
  That might the gift deserve.
Concealed from every sight,
  I wore this gem of art,
I hung it round my neck,
  And hid it on my heart.
For years and years I tried
  A fitting hand to find,
And to the anxious search
  I gave up heart and mind.

Whene'er I met with one
  Who seemed of worth indeed,
I took mysterious ways
  Her very soul to read;
And more to prove her heart,
  My heart to her I gave,
And waited on her wish,
  A pleased and willing slave.
But ere upon her hand
  The ring its glory shed,
Her love in something failed,
  And mine forever fled!

One came at last, who seemed
  To live for me alone,
To never have a wish
  Or will, except my own:
Her smile around me shone
  As soft as summer skies,
And all the light of heaven
  Looked on me from her eyes.
I tried her love and truth,
  In every way I could;
But firm her love remained,
  Her truth unshaken stood.
"The fitting hand is found,"
  I said, "Thou charm divine!
And in a fitting time
  Thy light shall on it shine!

Then fortune's rarest gifts
  Shall wait upon her lot;
And beauty that will last,
  And fame that fadeth not!"
Well pleased, I wandered forth,
  To muse on this alone—
When crashing to my heart,
  There came a little stone!
And whose the careless hand
  By which the stone was hurled?
Oh, say it was not hers!
  Not hers, of all the world!
Alas! the hand was hers
  From which the missile flew!
It shattered my poor heart!
  The ring was shivered, too!

## THE STORY OF A KING.

DEDICATED TO AN EMPEROR.

"What are those people reading?"
  Said Frederick, half aloud,
As looking from his window
  He saw an eager crowd.

One of his six-foot soldiers
  Who heard him, answered, "Sire!
Your Majesty permitting,
  I hasten to inquire."

He soon returned: "Oh, Sire!
  'T is horrible to see!
'T is an atrocious libel
  Upon your Majesty!"

"A libel!" said the monarch,
  And paused with thoughtful frown—
"Shall I disperse the people?"—
  "No—merely take it down."

"Yes, Sire!"—"Friend, stop a moment—
You'll take it down, indeed—
But just to place it lower,
So all with ease may read."

The soldier stood bewildered,
But from the monarch's eye
He caught a hidden meaning,
And left without reply.

When he removed the paper
They watched with sullen eyes,
But when he placed it lower,
They stood in hushed surprise.

"Now read at your convenience—
The king would have it so,
Content to ask his people
Are these things true or no?"

They spurned away the libel
Which now had lost its weight—
A thunder rose to heaven—
"Live Frederick the Great!"

Now this was not the weakness
Of a good-natured fool—
It was the manly wisdom
Of one that knew to rule.

Thou who to France hast given
  Her former power and glory,
Complete thy own, by taking
  The moral of my story.

Trust in thyself aud people—
  In chains and exile less—
To take the sting from libels,
  *Give freedom to the press!*

## WHAT I WOULD LIKE.

I AM a very moderate man,
Of moderate fortune, too:
I 've forty dollars, and I think
A little more would do.
I only wish to buy a house,
Where fashion holds her sway,
And furnish it with all that best
Becomes the present day.
A carriage I would like to have,
And horses, two or four;
But forty dollars will not pay—
I 'd like a little more.
Sculptures aud paintings I would like,
The best of every time;
And books by thousands,—all the good
Of every age and clime.
Grand parties I would like to give
To fifty thousand bores,
And hand my purse to borrowing friends,
(God knows they come by scores.)

I 'd like to win the ladies' hearts
  With presents they adore,
But forty dollars won't do that—
  I 'd like a little more.
And something of less selfish aim
  Should also share my wealth,
The ragged I would like to clothe,
  And give to sickness health.
I 'd like to give the foreign thieves
  And beggars, every day,
By thousands, pours upon our shores,
  The means——to go away.
I 'd like to make my friends all rich,
  And all the nation blest;
But forty dollars will not do—
  *Who offers me the rest?*

## THE PEOPLE'S PRINCES.

As I was sauntering through the street,
  In mood half thoughtful and half merry,
I chanced a barefoot boy to meet,
  Ragged, and very dirty—very.

His brow was dark with grief—and dirt—
  Unknown to joy or Croton water—
Yet Nature made him fair and bright
  As any rich man's son or daughter.

Slight fragment of humanity,
  Unnoticed by thy luckier brothers!
I wonder what thy lot will be,
  And what its bearing upon others!

Just now my dog is more account,
  Who snapping at thy bare heels follows;—
Those would not give a cent for thee,
  Would bid for him a hundred dollars!

That girl in gold and gems arrayed,
  Some "curled darling of our nation,"
Who glances at thee half afraid,
  Would think thy touch a degradation.

That simpering fop, more girlish still,
  Dressed up as for a world's inspection,
Averts his face with quickening pace,
  As if he thought thy sight infection.

No matter—thou hast mind and soul
  Within thy form's unsightly prison;
And these may urge thee yet to rise,
  As many a mighty man has risen.

Do wash thy face!—so I may trace
  Some glimpses of thy future story;
Who knows but fate may grace thee yet
  With youth and beauty, wealth and glory!

Oh, then, that girl who shuns thee now,
  May seek in thee her joy or sorrow;
That fop may boast himself thy friend,
  And come like mine—to fawn and borrow!

That as it may—the humblest child
  I reverence, though in dirt and tatters,
As equal in the sight of God
  With any prince that fortune flatters.

For ye are princes, Little Ones!
  Heirs of the Kingdom of Salvation!
Your heavenly birthright keep in view,
  No matter what your earthly station!

## TWENTY YEARS AGO.

I MET a girl the other day,
  Some twelve years old, or so,
The image of a nymph I loved
  Some twenty years ago.

The blushing cheek, the sparkling eye,
  The hair of raven flow,—
Ah, how they set my heart a-blaze
  Some twenty years ago!

I spoke—her answers did not much
  Of wit or wisdom show—
But thus the lovely Flora talked
  Some twenty years ago.

What! could a shallow girl like this
  My heart in tumult throw?
I must have been a little green
  Some twenty years ago!

I 've met the lovely Flora since—
  Her charms have vanished, though—
Her wit and wisdom are—the same
  As twenty years ago!

I look upon that faded cheek,
  Unlit by feeling's glow;
And thank her that she scorned my love
  Some twenty years ago!

Fond boy! who now wouldst gladly die
  To please some simpering Miss—
God knows what *thou* wilt think of *her*
  Some twenty years from this!

---

## THE INFLUENCE OF THE AFFECTIONS.

The beautiful humanities
  Of Nature in the simplest dress,
Speak to our sweetest sympathies
  Far more than language can express.
I saw a ragged little boy
  Run to a withered dame's embrace,
To welcome her with bounding joy,
  And fondly press her haggard face.
Her shabby garment to his eyes
  Is rich; her withered face is fair;
For they are hers—and she supplies
  His perished mother's love and care.
The world is full of pain and harm,
  And life at best is little worth;
Yet pure affection is a charm
  That almost makes a heaven of earth.

## SONG OF THE TOOTHACHE IMPS.

Sometimes about a hollow tooth
We dance around, around the mouth;
Thither the throbbing torture comes,
And ague swelling doleful gums:
Sometimes we dance through bone and brain
To howls of rage and yells of pain,
And when with patient men we meet,
We dance—to the stamping of their feet.
At the wight's raving, dismal voice,
When others tremble we rejoice,
And nimbly, nimbly, dance we still
To the echoes from the horrid thrill!*

*SONG OF THE WITCHES.

"Sometimes about a hollow tree,
Around, around, around, dance we;
Thither the chirping cricket comes,
And beetles singing drowsy hums;
Sometimes we dance o'er ferns and furze
To howls of wolves and barks of curs;
And when with none of these we meet,
We dance—to the echoes of our feet!
At the night-raven's dismal voice,
When others tremble we rejoice:
And nimbly, nimbly dance we still
To the echoes from a hollow hill!"—Macbeth.

## THE WET MORNING.

Equipped with silk umbrella,
  And broadcloth overcoat,
With overshoes and leggins,
  And muffled to the throat,
Forth from a plenteous table,
  Where he could nothing eat,
Steps Midas to his carriage,
  And takes his lordly seat.
The sleek and pompous coachman,
  The footman spruce and proud,
Attend upon him, cringing,
  Among the cringing crowd;
Yet on his cheek is fever,
  And on his brow a frown,
As off he rides, the richest
  And saddest man in town!

Barefooted and bareheaded,
  His garments torn and thin,
His heart as free from sorrow
  As ours should be from sin;
Fresh from some scanty table,
  Where, well content, he fed,
Perhaps on bad potatoes,
  Perhaps on crusts of bread;

Flushed high, not with the wine-cup,
  But with his youthful blood;
Regardless of the rain-drops,
  Unconscious of the mud;
Forth bounds the little Gamin,
  And trolls his hoop along,
With now a careless whistle,
  And now a snatch of song.
His jacket flung wide open,
  His bosom bare and brown,
He runs, the ragged rascal,
  The happiest wight in town!

With many cares and troubles
  It tasks my strength to bear,
I look on many pleasures
  I may not hope to share:
Yet finds the serpent, envy,
  No shelter in my breast—
Let theirs be power and glory,
  Who have deserved them best;
Let theirs be wealth and grandeur—
  Who best deserve—or not—
My own may be as happy,
  Although an humbler lot;
And still to every station
  That Fate awards below,
She gives its compensation,
  If we could only know!

And to the least among us
  God sends some blessing down,
That leaves no cause to envy
  The greatest man in town!

Then go! ye dreams of glory!
  Of fortune, hopes as vain!
Farewell, ye smiles of beauty!
  So youth and health remain!
Ah! Time, remorseless, whispers,
  "Farewell to youth and health!"
Rejoice, poor little Gamin!
  For thine, a priceless wealth!
And one who would not envy
  The laurel or the crown,
Might envy little Gamin,
  The happiest wight in town!

## LIFE AND DEATH.

FROM THE GERMAN.

Life is the hot and garish sun—
  Death the refreshing night.—
Come darkness! I am sleepy now
  And weary of the light!

There springs a tree above my bed—
  A bird amid it gleams—
It sings aloud—it sings of love—
  I hear it in my dreams.

## BOOTH.

Just now it came into my head,
I know not how it came,
That somewhere I have heard or read,
That Junius Brutus Booth was dead,
An actor of some fame.

In Richard he was really great,
Though Kean's was lauded higher:
All parts, when not in tipsy state,
He played with judgment accurate,
With spirit, force, and fire.

His tragic powers high praise bespeak—
His comic claim as high;
Profound in the absurd or weak,
He made you laugh in Jerry Sneak,
And almost made you cry!

For to his sense, with feeling rife,
The "fun" was not the best—
That tragedy of common life,
The loving fool, the tyrant wife,
He deemed a *serious* jest.

He was a scholar deeply versed
In old and modern lore;

A poet, too, and not the worst;
His lines, when by himself rehearsed,
Were seldom thought a bore.

At HOLLAND'S lodgings once we met—
Our speech on trifles ran—
The nothings that we soon forget,
But leaves me an impression yet
Of "wit and gentleman."

A bard, the humblest of our times,
While sauntering down the street,
Together strung these careless rhymes,
And thought how oft ambition climbs
As poor reward to meet!

What lasts of BOOTH?—a paragraph
Some flippant paper gives;—
A lie, or only true by half,
To set on barren fools to laugh—
And thus his "glory" lives!

Green boy, who seest on the stage
Some bully foam and roar,
And thinkest it glorious to engage
Applause, by shamming grief or rage,
Go——be a fool no more!

Few idols of the box or pit
Might well with BOOTH compare;

A genius, scholar, poet, wit,
For every range of talent fit—
And Booth is what?—and where?

In vain his mind was heaven-inspired,
By study, too, refined—
All nature gave, or art acquired,
Was only for the hour admired,
And then it passed from mind.

Life's real scenes should be thy stage—
Act well and nobly there—
Subdue thy passions, curb their rage—
Thou mayest not man's applause engage—
But that of angels share!

---

## THE SUM OF PHILOSOPHY.

Do fortune's smiles upon thee wait,
With honor, power, and high estate,
Let not thy heart be too elate—
All this shall pass away.
Art thou the sport of fortune's hate,
Forsaken, poor, and desperate,
Still bear the worst with mind sedate;
All this shall pass away.
Our joys and pains are brief in date;
The deeds we do of good and great,
Alone survive our mortal state,
And never pass away.

# THE HERO.

INSCRIBED TO JAMES B. K——.

Let others sing of deeds of arms
  By heroes who have ravaged earth,
Who shook the world with war's alarms,
  While death and carnage crowned their worth;

A nobler hero claims my song
  Than we on history's page may find;
Not his the fame of doing wrong—
  He lives a blessing to mankind.

A blessing and a martyr, too—
  For them all comfort he forsakes;
When others for assistance sue,
  From friends and family he breaks.

He leaves his food, he leaves his sleep,
  E'en in the deadest hour of night,
Though floods descend and tempests sweep,
  And heaven denies one gleam of light.

Through storm and darkness on he goes,
  To hut or hall—no matter where;
Intent to soothe the sufferer's woes,
  And save the mourner from despair.

Scenes he must view that break his heart,
  And deeds perform his blood that chill;
But so that he may good impart,
  He acts as with an iron will.

And he must bear with vain complaints,
  When Nature makes the progress slow;
But with a patience worthy saints,
  Will still his needful cares bestow.

Alike to palaces of wealth,
  Or hovels where the friendless pine,
He carries comfort, life, and health,
  As if a messenger divine.

For this *his* comfort up he gave,
  For this *his* health is often lost,
And oft another's life to save
  The peril of *his* life has cost.

Who is this hero, who may claim
  The world's applause and that of heaven?
Ah, friend! if I should breathe thy name,
  No other answer need be given!

All *good* physicians share the praise—
  May worthy honors on them fall!
But thou who hast prolonged my days,
  I fain would praise thee more than all!

But not for praise didst thou impart
  Thy aid, or any selfish ends;
Yet take this tribute of my heart,
  Best of physicians and of friends!

## WHAT SHOULD WE DO, MY BROTHER?

Where pleasant fields are growing,
  Where rocks are tossed on high,
Where streams in music flowing,
  Delight the ear and eye,
Where rivalling each other,
  Fair scenes invite our choice,
What should we do, my brother?
  Rejoice! we should rejoice!

Where woods in tangled wildness
  Oppose our weary way,
Where bowers in shady mildness
  Invite a sweet delay;
Where wild birds to each other
  Their blithesome carols voice,
What should we do, my brother?
  Rejoice! we should rejoice!

When slowly home returning,
  While moonlight's golden streams
Refresh the brow still burning
  With day's departing beams;
While cheering on each other
  With songs of merry voice,
What should we do, my brother?
  Rejoice! we should rejoice!

## THE CANARY BIRD.

Thine is a lovely song, my bird!
Though by thy mates 't is never heard,
And it may seem to those around
An idle, though a pleasant sound;
For not to them is given to know
The feelings whence thy carols flow.
Bird! thou art severed from thy kind,
And in a narrow cage confined,
Whose bars obscure the fields of light
Which once alone could bound thy flight,
Of which the glimpses serve at most
To mock the freedom thou hast lost;
Yet, bird, thy heart is brave and strong,
Companioned only by thy song,
Which careless if 't is heard or not,
Sheds light and beauty on thy lot;
The gift of God thou dost employ,
And in its use dost find thy joy.

Like thine how oft the poet's fate;
How lone it seems—how desolate!

No kindred spirit near to share
The feelings which he wastes on air;
No heart in which he can awake
Responsive chords to thrill or break!
Life's fettering cares around him cling,
And bind to earth his heavenly wing,
And from his vision half efface
The skies which are his native place.
His proudest lay is heard by few,
Nor meets from those the honor due,
But to the kindest seems to be
A beauty—but a mystery!—
Yet though it may not win him fame,
Or love, his more exalted aim,
His godlike thoughts will have their voice,
And in that glorious sound rejoice,
As mounting heaven, it peals along,
To God as a thanksgiving song!

## YOUNG NAPOLEON AT HIS FATHER'S GRAVE.

FROM THE GERMAN OF SAPHIR.

THE king of Rome in slumber
  In Schonbrun's garden lies;
Sees not the light of heaven,
  Sees not the vaulted skies;
Far on a foreign island
  Reclines Napoleon;
Lies not with his own people,
  Lies not beside his son;
Lies not amid his marshals,
  The pillars of his throne,
Lies not among his soldiers,
  In Europe, once his own;
But buried deep in darkness,
  Mid circling seas and skies,
Chained to a rock forever
  The dead Prometheus lies.

Where scorching sunbeams wither
  Trunk, leaf, and branch, and all,
The mighty Emperor slumbers,
  "The Little Corporal!

No flowers above him flourish,
  No cypress branches wave;
In sight of all creation,
  No pilgrim seeks his grave.

Thus many years he slumbers,
  Deserted and alone;
When hark! there comes at midnight
  A knock upon the stone;
A knock—a gentle whisper,
  But of no mortal breath:
"Wake up! wake up! thou hero!
  Wake from the sleep of death!"
Another knock and whisper:
  "Rise mighty Emperor!
Here to thy court with tidings
  Comes Earth's ambassador!"
Another knock and whisper:
  "Rise father! take me home!
My soul has come in lightning!
  Thy only child has come!"

Earth crumbles—marble sunders,
  And heaves aside the lid,
That long of the dead hero
  The awful ashes hid;
And then its fleshless finger
  Th' imperial corpse extends,

To show his heir of glory
  His empire's farthest ends.

"Look down into my palace,
  My dear, my only son!
Again do I behold thee,
  My child—Napoleon!
Survey the ground beneath me,
  The walls on either hand;
The length and breadth thou seest
  Of all thy father's land!"
Then hand in hand they grappled
  In skeleton embrace;
And lip to lip caressing,
  They nestled face to face;
The grave closed in that moment
  On father and on son;
And vanished in that moment
  The House-Napoleon!

## NEW-YEAR THOUGHTS.

How many are now in the cold grave reposing
  Who welcomed the dawn of the year that has fled!
How little, alas! did they think that its closing
  Should find them inurned in the home of the dead!
How many this year to the grave's dark dominions
  Shall hasten, who welcome its rising career,
Ere time once again on his air-feathered pinions
  Shall usher the dawn of another New-Year!

And I, who now muse on the thousands departed,
  May follow them ere the return of this day,
Bedewed with the tears of some friend broken-hearted,
  Who now smiles upon me, unthinking and gay;
And better than I should survive to deplore them,
  The few that to share my affections remain,
Oh, better by far I should perish before them,
  Nor hail the return of the New-Year again!

How sad to be torn from our friends and connexions,
  And hid in the valley of darkness alone!
What comfort to hope their surviving affections
  Shall cherish our image on memory's throne!
The hearts that now love me, will they not regret me?
  Will ever my memory cease to be dear?
The friends of my bosom—oh! can they forget me,
  If swept from their sight by the close of the year?

## A HUNDRED YEARS FROM NOW.

WHAT millions live to-day
As they might ever stay,
How soon to pass away!
  Sweet face and lofty brow,
So pleasant now to see—
Alas! where will they be
  A hundred years from now?

The sage with silver hair,
Proud youth and maiden fair,
Time will not pause to spare—
  Glad childhood's sunny brow,
The infant's dimpling face—
All gone without a trace,
  A hundred years from now!

The ills we scarce sustain,
The trouble and the pain
That vex the heart and brain,
  And wring the calmest brow—

All serious as they seem,
Fade, a forgotten dream,
  A hundred years from now!

The time seems far away,
Yet will not long delay,
It comes with every day
  That goes, we know not how!
Howe'er thy lot be cast,
'T is all the same at last,
  A hundred years from now.

In all but *this* the same—
Some few may leave a name,
A monument of fame
  That time shall never bow;
Or heavenly-thoughted page,
To consecrate our age
  A hundred years from now!

## VANITY OF VANITIES.

VANITY of vanities!
  All the joys of earth,
Vanity of vanities!
  Are of little worth.
Vanity of vanities!
  Wealth and grandeur high,
Vanity of vanities!
  Small the bliss they buy!
Vanity of vanities!
  Sweetest woman's smile,
Vanity of vanities!
  Charms but for a while!
Vanity of vanities!
  Glory's loudest blast,
Vanity of vanities!
  Dulls the ear at last!
Vanity of vanities!
  What is life at best?
Vanity of vanities!
  All but death's a jest!

## NEW-YEAR HYMN.

THANKS to our Heavenly FATHER!
  Though angels tune his praise,
He will permit His children
  Their humbler song to raise:
Thanks to our Heavenly FATHER,
  Whose love sustains us here,
And spares us yet to welcome
  Another happy year!

For all the years departed,
  For all the years to come,
For all the thousand blessings
  That crown our happy home:
For all our loving kindred,
  For all the friends we claim,
We thank our Heavenly FATHER,
  And bless His holy name!

## SPRING IS COMING.

SPRING is coming! Spring is coming!
Birds are chirping, insects humming;
Flowers are peeping from their sleeping;
Streams, escaped from winter's keeping,
In delighted freedom rushing,
Dance along in music gushing,
Scenes of late in deadness saddened,
Smile in animation gladdened:
All is beauty, all is mirth,
All is glory upon earth:
Shout we then with Nature's voice,
"Welcome, Spring! rejoice! rejoice!"

Spring is coming! come, my brother,
Let us wander with each other
To our well remembered wildwood,
Flourishing in Nature's childhood,
Where a thousand birds are singing,
And a thousand flowers are springing,
Where the dancing sunbeams quiver
On the forest-shaded river;
Let our youth of feeling out
To the youth of Nature shout,
While the hills repeat our voice—
Welcome, Spring! rejoice! rejoice!"

## MY PRETTY BIRDS.

My pretty birds, as sweet your song,
And of as blithesome kind,
As when you winged your flight along,
By but the skies confined;
Though severed from your native bowers,
And caged in narrow space,
As gay ye carol through your hours
As in your native place.

And grateful to the tender hand
That watches o'er your need,
Your little hearts with love expand,
While from that hand ye feed;
And this is well—ye need not mourn
The scenes that ye have lost,
For there the pangs ye might have borne
Of famine or of frost.

But man less wise—restrained from ill
By the Almighty's bars,
The rage to have his erring will
His spirit's music jars.
My birds, my sweet philosophers,
May I your wisdom learn,
And welcoming what God confers,
To His protection turn.

## MY CAP.

My cap! my well-worn leather cap;
  Though time has dimmed thy glossy hue,
Though broken hangs thy useless strap,
  And spots obscure thy band of blue,
I would not give thee for the best
  That graces fashion's votary;
So long hast thou my brow caressed,
  Thou hast become a part of me;

And happy thoughts, of better worth,
  Are born in thy obscure embrace,
Than any diadem of earth
  Encircles in its resting-place.
With thee on my unhonored head,
  I con the page of mystic lore,
Explore the light by genius shed,
  And gather wisdom's precious ore.

For years, in every scene of pride
  Or joy that it was mine to tread,
My chosen friend was at my side,
  And thou, my cap! upon my head;

And thus we rambled many a mile,
  To witness Nature's wildest charms,
To revel in her glorious smile,
  Or worship her sublime alarms.

We braved the tempest's furious shock,
  In shivering night, or burning day;
Headlong we leaped from rock to rock,
  Or through the forest toiled our way;
Or wandered where the rivers glide
  In darkness by the tangled cliff,
Or tossed upon their swelling tide
  That sobbed around the shuddering skiff!

With Jerome thou hast seen me share
  All the communion friendship knows,
The wildest hope, the deepest care,
  The brightest joys, the darkest woes:
To him, then, when I must depart,
  To lay my head on Nature's lap,
For kingdom I 'd bequeath my heart,
  For diadem—my leather cap!

## THE SUN.

Come forth, thou glorious sun!
  And brighten up the skies,
And smile the world upon,
  Whose life is in thine eyes!
Thou beautiful and bright!
  Come to thy throne of day,
Within whose mellow light
  My soul would melt away!

He comes! he comes! he blesses
  Creation like a god;
And flings his golden tresses
  Of glory all abroad!
Look up, my soul, forsaken,
  But now, by every one,
To greet thy friend, awaken—
  The sun! the lovely sun!

## A WOMAN AS SHE SHOULD BE.

In person decent, and in dress,
Her manners and her words express
The decency of mind;
Good humor brightens up her face,
Where passion never leaves a trace,
Nor frowns a look unkind.
No vexing sneer, no angry word,
No scandal from her lips is heard,
Where truth and sweetness blend;
Submission to her husband's will,
Her study is to please him still,
His fond and faithful friend.
She watches his returning way,
When from the troubles of the day
He seeks a home of bliss;
She runs to meet him with a smile,
And if no eye be near the while,
The smile is with a kiss!

## FORGET ME NOT.

When I am in that distant place
Where I must dwell awhile,
How will I miss thy pleasant face,
And its bewitching smile!
Thy image will pursue me there
Through each sequestered spot—
And oh that mine thy thoughts may share!
Sweet friend! forget me not!

In thee 't was mine to recognize
One of no common kind—
One look into each other's eyes,
And mind replied to mind!
And still thy spirit walks with mine,
Though far apart our lot,
And still my soul repeats to thine—
"Sweet friend! forget me not!"

How brief our friendship's date appears!
And yet it seems to me
As if we had been friends for years,
As we for life shall be!
And when, by Fate's remorseless will,
I meet the common lot,
I ask not for thy tears—but still,
Sweet friend!—forget me not!

**DELISSER & PROCTER,**

(Successors to Stanford & Swords,)

No. 508 BROADWAY,

HAVE RECENTLY PUBLISHED

# THE LIFE OF ROBERT BURNS;

BY CARLYLE,

AND OTHERS, FORMING THE SECOND VOLUME OF

## THE HOUSEHOLD LIBRARY,

18mo. Cloth, 50 cents.

"Nothing truly great has ever been written of Burns, except this sketch of Carlyle's. It is genius comprehending genius. One can read it, and always with increasing admiration."—*N. Y. Day Book.*

"This spirited portrait by Carlyle is one of the grandest efforts of the pen of that great writer."—*Commercial Advertiser.*

"It is by far the finest estimate of Robert Burns as a man and a poet, that has ever been written. No man capable of appreciating Burns, can fail to admire this noble essay, which, among compositions of the kind, is, perhaps, without its equal."—*Scottish American.*

"Carlyle's famous portraiture of Burns was written when he wrote his best."—*Evening Post.*

"Every Scotsman and lover of true poetry will not fail to possess himself of a copy of this eloquent tribute. We heartily welcome this most opportune contribution to our literature."—*Frank Leslie's Paper.*

"Full of gems, we can cordially recommend the book to the literary student, and to all who love a good mental meal."—*N. Y. News.*

***** Copies sent to any address prepaid on receipt of the price.**

## THE HOUSEHOLD LIBRARY

will consist of 12 Vols., 50 cents each, and will comprise works of the highest historical and literary excellence—among others, the following:—

**Vol. I. Life and Martrydom of Joan of Arc.** BY MICHELET.
**II. Life of Robert Burns.** BY CARLYLE AND OTHERS.
**III. Life and Times of Socrates.** BY GROTE.
**IV. Life of Columbus.** BY LAMARTINE.
**V. Life of Frederick the Great.** BY MACAULAY.
**VI. Life of Peter the Great.**
**VII. Life of Mahomet.** BY GIBBON AND OTHERS.
**VIII. Life of Luther.** BY CHEV. BUNSEN &C.

It has long been a desideratum that a judicious selection of works of sterling merit, and solid instruction, should be produced in attractive form, and at a price that would place them within the reach of every family circle. This excellent series is especially adapted for the perusal of families, young men, and all who seek to combine intellectual and moral improvement with the fascinations of literature.

I.—SECOND EDITION.

# CHRONICLES OF THE BASTILE.

Six Hundred and Seventy Octavo Pages.

**Sixteen superb Engravings, designed by Cruikshank, and engraved by Bross.** Cloth, $2.00.

IT CONTAINS A DESCRIPTION OF—

The Old Man of the Bastile—Thrilling Scenes in the Bastile—The Haunts of the Conspirators—The Secret Meetings of the Lutetians—Louis Quatorze—Duc d'Orleans—Louis XVI—Madame de Maintenon—Marie Antoinette—The Man of the Iron Mask—Jacques, the Spy—D'Argenson, Governor of the Bastile—Murat—Mirabeau—Foulin—Robespierre—The Compact of Liberty—The Gathering of the Lutetians—The Revolutionary Clubs—The Great Revolution—The Destruction of the Bastile.

As a revelation of crime and suffering, these 'Chronicles' have acquired a grand and solemn value.—*Christian Intelligencer.*

In all history there is no parallel to the Bastile for terrible romance.—*Scot. Amer.*

It is stronger and more absorbing in interest than any amount of fiction the author could have called to his aid. It is, indeed, a chapter in French history written in blood. This work will go out over the land to excite hate of oppression and wrong in the hearts of all who read it.—*Commercial Times.*

The scenes are among the most thrilling in the history of the world.—*Cin. Com.*

This exciting narrative is equal in interest to 'The Mysteries of Paris,' by EUGENE SUE.—*S. Courier.*

No one can examine this book without desiring to read it to the end, and with every page read the interest increases.—*N. H. Palladium.*

II.—FOURTH EDITION OF

**PEARLS OF THOUGHT,** RELIGIOUS AND PHILOSOPHICAL, Gathered from Old Authors. 18mo. cloth, 50 cents.

Fair pearls of wisdom, fully set forth in a goodly casket.—*Prot. Churchman.*

It is a little library of itself.—*Musical World.*

A very gem of a book; a companion for solitude, a feast for friends in company.—*Observer.*

A religious and literary treasure.—*Boston Post.*

It is a choice basket of rare old fruit, which time has only mellowed and sweetened.—*Independent.*

III.—UNIFORM WITH THE ABOVE—THE SIXTIETH EDITION,

**WORDS OF JESUS and FAITHFUL PROMISER.** By Rev. DR. MACDUFF, of Glasgow. 18mo. cloth, 38 cents.

A literary and religious luxury.—*Churchman.*

IV.

**LYRA GERMANICA; Hymns for the Sundays and chief Festivals of the Christian Year.** Translated from the German, by CATHARINE WINKWORTH. 12mo. Rubricated. cloth, antique, 75 cents.

"The best selection of sacred poetry, as illustrative of the Ritual, extant."

☞ *Copies of the above works sent to any address on receipt of prices named.*

DELISSER & PROCTER, *Publishers,*

508 BROADWAY, N. Y.

www.ingramcontent.com/pod-product-compliance
Lightning Source LLC
LaVergne TN
LVHW050520100826
845148LV00002B/401

* 9 7 8 1 4 2 5 5 2 0 7 4 8 *